12-16-97

THIS IS LOVE

This Is Love

~~~~~~

By Rev. M. Raymond, o.c.s.o.

THE BRUCE PUBLISHING COMPANY • MILWAUKEE

NIHIL OBSTAT:

FR. M. CHARLES ENGLISH, O.C.S.O.
FR. M. THOMAS AQUINAS PORTER, O.C.S.O.
Censores Ordinis

IMPRIMI POTEST:

MOST REV. DOM M. GABRIEL SORTAIS, O.C.S.O.
Abbas Generalis

NIHIL OBSTAT:

REV. JOHN F. MURPHY, S.T.D.
Censor Librorum

IMPRIMATUR:

✠ ROMAN R. ATKIELSKI, D.D.
Ep. Aux. et Vicarius Generalis Milwauchiensis
die 24ª novembris, 1963

Unless otherwise noted, the Scripture texts used in this book
are from the Kleist-Lilly edition of the New Testament, and
from the Knox edition of the Old Testament.

Library of Congress Catalog Card Number: 64–14802

© 1964 THE BRUCE PUBLISHING COMPANY

MADE IN THE UNITED STATES OF AMERICA

TO

THE IMMACULATE HEART OF MARY

WHICH WAS PIERCED BENEATH HIS ALTAR AND
OFFERED IN HIS MASS

AND TO

THE LEONARDS ALL

FOR THE WAY
THEY ARE MAKING HIS MASS THEIR LIFE — AND
THEIR LIVES HIS MASS.

CONTENTS

THIS IS LOVE

"Father, how can I get more out of Mass?"

Dear Lord, that question has come too often of late! And from many different quarters. Laymen have asked it, both the so-called unlearned and those who have been highly educated. Religious have asked it, both male and female, cloistered and active, as well as those in what is called the "mixed life." Even priests have asked it.

Does it please You, Lord, and pain You, as it pains and pleases me?

I thrill to find so many members of our one Body coming in, as it were, from the periphery of existence, and seeking to plunge into the center and source of our life. I thrill to see them placing their fingers on what is the pulsing Heart of our being: Your Heart — and You who are our all. It is thrilling, Lord, to find so many actually making Mass their very lives, and their lives veritable Masses. For what else is Christian life and living if it is not doing what You have done and yet do?

That is something not all realize, Lord. Yet Paul's words are unmistakably clear: *semper vivens ad interpellandum pro nobis* — You are living "to make intercession on our behalf" (Heb 7:25). This statement in the middle of this Epistle, which is so expressly on Your Priesthood and Your Sacrifice, should tell all just how You intercede. But if there are any who would doubt, Your beloved Disciple John makes it unquestionable in his Apocalypse. For he tells us that he saw You "standing in front of the throne . . . a Lamb as if slain" (5:6) and he heard the chant of Heaven. It is a Mass chant: "Holy, Holy, Holy is the Lord God Almighty" (4:8). Since this is the way it is with You who are God's Christ,

1

must it not be the same with all of us who call ourselves Christians? Indeed it *is* "Mass that matters," Lord — and practically nothing else does ultimately.

So I thrill to the question.

Yet, what so thrills can also pain, because so much lies implicit in the very positing of the query. I saw this recently, Lord, when a man who is not only a university graduate, but a university professor, came to me and said: "Father, I do not know how to become holy through Mass." He was being honest. But his honesty hurt. He was also burningly sincere. And it was his sincerity that helped me over the hurt, and set me planning these pages. For with an earnestness that spoke to me of hunger in his soul, he added: "Can't you tell me how?"

Requests such as these, Lord, have me reliving the night You made Mass possible. Thanks to John the Beloved it is easy to recapture that scene; for he has given us chapters that pulse with life and throb with love. For once Judas had gone into the night, John narrates happenings which show that You became different. You not only talked fondly, freely, lovingly with Your Eleven, but You sounded like a Man outside Yourself with joy, a Man in ecstasy. You spoke to, and of, Your Father in such a manner that You set the men in the Cenacle chattering. Peter had his say. So did Thomas.

But it is Philip's request, and Your reply, that hold me whenever I am faced with questions on Mass that cause both pleasure and pain; for Philip's remark seems to have affected You the same way.

You had been telling Thomas that You are the way, the truth, and the life; that no one comes to the Father except through You, when Philip broke in with the plea: "Master, let us see the Father, and we shall be satisfied" (Jn 14:6–8). He did not realize all he was asking, of that I am sure. For, actually, he was requesting Heaven — and its essential bliss. Yet You, who told us again and again that You had come to lead us to the Father, were pained by Philip's petition. Why, Lord? Your reply cannot be called a rebuke; it is spoken too softly, too kindly, with too much gentleness and love. Yet I find it weighted with sadness. I hear weariness in Your voice, Lord, as You say: "Philip, so long a time have I been in your midst, and you do not know me?" That is a puzzling question. How could Philip have known that You and the Father were, and are, one? Had You remained in their midst years longer, would they have known? Your oneness with the Father is mystery at its most mysterious.

At first blush I would have taken Philip's request as something that would have thrilled You, Lord. And yet . . . well, the episode gives me some semblance of a parallel with this question about Mass.

Dear Lord, there are times when this Christian life of ours seems so utterly simple that when educated Catholics approach me with a question such as the present one, I secretly wonder if You have not sent some new Isaias to "dull the hearts of this people, . . . deaden their ears, dazzle their eyes, so that they cannot see with those eyes, hear with those ears, understand with that heart, and turn back to You and win healing" (cf. Is 6:9, 10).

Why do I think such a thing? Because, Lord, in Mass You are present to us as really — although it be mystically, sacramentally — as You were to those in the Cenacle physically. You look at us and see us as clearly as You saw Peter, James, and John that night. You speak to us as directly as You spoke to Philip. You can be touched intimately, and even more intimately than You were when John laid his head on Your breast. And yet . . . well, Lord, I know Mass is *Mysterium Fidei* — *the* Mystery of our Faith — but often, the faith of those who ask about Mass presents me with a greater mystery. They do not look — and see; they do not listen — and hear; they do not touch — and taste *YOU*. So help me now to help them.

First of all, Lord, let me be as intimate and informal in this book as one can be, and should be, in a personal letter. Let heart speak to heart. I would not think of speaking of Mass any other way, Lord; for You are Mass — and You are Love.

John the Evangelist once did precisely what I long to do now; and did it for the identical purpose. Hence, I borrow the opening of his first Epistle as perfect opening for this book, and say: "We proclaim what was from the beginning, what we have heard, what we have seen with our own eyes, what we have gazed upon, and what we have embraced with our own hands. I refer to the Word who is and who imparts life. Indeed, this Life has manifested himself. We ourselves have seen and testify and proclaim that Eternal Life which was with the Father and has manifested himself. To you we proclaim what we have seen and heard, that you may share our treasure with us. That treasure is union with the Father and his Son, Jesus Christ. I write this to you that we may have joy in the fullest measure" (1 Jn 1:1–4).

There it is, Lord, the *finis operis* as well as the *finis operantis:* I would have this book give its every reader *joy* — and joy "in fullest measure." I would have that measureless joy come and consist in that "union with the Father and His Son" John speaks of; understanding always "in the unity of the Holy Spirit." For that is life's ultimate whether we consider life in its temporal, transient, ever changing phase, or in its fixity of eternity's endlessness. Was not that the final purpose of all Your work, and all Your working, Lord? You wanted us to have that joy which alone can satisfy, and You wanted us to have it in its fullness. That is why You offered Your Mass, and why You made it possible for us to offer ours. That we might have this joy not only in the never passing "Now" of eternity, but in every passing now of time, You offered Yourself once in a bloody manner, and made it possible for us to offer You in an unbloody manner not only yesterday, today, and tomorrow, but all the day long down through the centuries, eras, epochs, and aeons until suns burn out and skies are fugitives.

I thank You for that, Lord. But now from my heart I plead: Let me be simplicity itself. I make this plea with burning earnestness, Lord; for I find our present-day world filled to the full with sophistication. We stifle, Lord, actually battle for every breath because of our oversophistication. I call it that deliberately, Lord;

for I know it is not wisdom. Almost everywhere there is smartness, glibness, cleverness, even brilliance. But where is there sincerity, solidity, substance? Where is there truth and wisdom? What Juvenal said of *Probitas* in his day, I dare to say of *Sapientia* in our day: *Laudatur et alget* — "It is praised, but it is left out in the cold." Actually, Wisdom is lonely and unloved. And precisely, Lord, because our sophisticates scorn that godlike quality called *simplicity.*

Our subject matter is anything but simple, Lord. But that does not deny us the possibility of presenting it with a clarity that comes from utter simplicity. One need but model on You in literature as in life. You made the abstract lucidly clear, because You were masterly in Your simplicity. Mass is a Mystery; but no more mysterious than Your divine providence. Yet You clarified that beyond all possibility of obscurity by pointing to the birds in the air and the flowers in the fields. What could be more simple? Then there are Your parables. With these You made the profoundest and most intangible of truths as intelligible and familiar as one's own name. That is the type of simplicity I am praying for, Lord; for, with it, we can enable all classes of people to get ever deeper insights into this sublime Mystery called Mass. That "we" is not editorial, Lord. It is factual. For I am ever mindful of that teaching of Yours: "Without me, you can do nothing" (Jn 15:5). Be with me now. Then I will exemplify that other truth which is antistrophe to Your strophe; I will be able to say with St. Paul: "I can do all things in him who strengthens me" (Phil 4:13).

To this same Paul You once said: "My grace is sufficient for you, for my power is made perfectly evident in your weakness" (2 Cor 12:9). Relying on that grace, and realizing full well my weakness, I long to make Your power "perfectly evident." Hence, I dare to address myself to this task which otherwise would be presumptuous.

Those who have asked me to show them how to get more out of Mass, Lord, need no dissertation on the history of the various rites, nor any essay on the development of rubrics. Neither would they be greatly helped by any profound analysis of the different prayers in, and parts of, Mass. They are already acquainted with the Missal, and know how to participate, externally at least, in the Sacred Liturgy. So our scope is limited, Lord, and our task comparatively light. But I would be remiss, aye, niggardly, did I not praise You, bless You, thank You, for having inspired Your scholars — Your apostles and true doctors of the present day — to write their magnificent works on what is "the chief act of divine worship" the "source and center of Christian piety," as Pius XII pointed out in his *Mediator Dei — Mass.*

I am thinking now, Lord, of such masterly works as that by Joseph A. Jungmann, S.J.: *The Mass of the Roman Rite.* Therein one can find a complete history of Mass from the first celebrated by You in the Cenacle down to the latest celebrated by You through Your priests this morning. I am thinking also of Canon A. Croegaert's work: *The Mass — A Liturgical Commentary.* How rightly that has been named "an encyclopedia on the Mass." I am thinking of those long shelves of recent books on our Holy Sacrifice, which range from scholarly researches into the origin and development of the Liturgy, down through studies on the symbols and signs used in Mass, and on to popular works of devotion on the Holy Eucharist. No one dare say there is a dearth of worthwhile books on this subject of ours; for practically every phase has been carefully covered by truly competent men.

May I thank You now, Lord, for men like Maurice de la Taille, S.J., Abbot, and Father Eugene Masure? These men have done marvelous work on the Eucharist. But any long excerpts from their splendid studies would be utterly out of place in this little effort of ours, Lord. I feel that our readers want something simple, substantial, personal, and practical. I believe we can give it to them, Lord, by using the wealth all these masters mined, but presenting it in our own simplified form.

Let me also praise You and thank You, Lord, for the grand growth of the Liturgical Movement. It has been gradual. Some might even say it has been slow. But slow growth most always means sound growth. You have been a Good Shepherd, Lord; You did not overdrive Your flock. Back in the nineteenth century You began to lead them by having Dom Gueranger at Solesmes rediscover, as it were, the doctrinal and devotional riches in the liturgy. It hurts to hear some sophisticated moderns criticize this good man. Of course his work was imperfect. What work of man is not? But that does not make it unworthy. Some are calling it "monastic," "antiquarian," "aesthetic," when they would be much more wise were they to call it "apostolic" and "pastoral." This good Abbot wanted to make the prayer of the Church the basis for the personal piety of all Christians. I thank You for the success You granted him, Lord. Forgive his critics.

Then came Your great St. Pius X with his restoration of frequent Communion and his pastoral effort to get the people to participate in their Holy Sacrifice. His remark that "active participation in the liturgy is the primary and indispensable source of the true Christian spirit" has become something of a landmark and a motto for the Movement, and a definite lead toward true Christian life and living. To implement this papal pronouncement, it would seem, You raised up Dom Lambert Beauduin. Because of his work in Belgium to have people use Missals, participate in dialogue Masses, base their lives on Calvary's rock, the empty Tomb, and Your place by the throne of the Father, I believe this man can be called the father of the modern Liturgical Movement which was so gloriously crowned by the *Mediator Dei* of Pius XII, and the decisions of Vatican II.

We will use passages from Pius' masterpiece, Lord, in order to ground our people solidly not only in the Liturgy but in the life of the Mystical Body. But I wonder if that classic would ever have been written if You had not inspired men like Abbot Ildefons Herwegen and his monks at Maria Laach. Thanks to their liturgical scholarship and deep, doctrinal reflections, riches have been discovered that in some way transform the theology of the Sacraments, and very especially that on the Eucharist. Of course there have been misgivings about some of their speculations. Undoubtedly some of them went too far. But hasn't that always been the way in the development of doctrine?

I praise You for Pius Parsch, for Matthias Joseph Scheeben, for Père Danielou, S.J., for Father de Lubac, S.J., and Yves Congar, O.P. I praise You for all who have given us new light, new insights, new ideas on Scripture, Tradition, Theology, Liturgy, and Christian living. But most of all I thank You, Lord, for Pius XII who restored the Paschal Vigil, changed the law on Eucharistic fast, allowed evening Mass, and taught us so fearlessly and well in his *Mediator Dei*.

I hope I have assimilated something from these masters, Lord, and that You will now enable me to present it in palatable form. The way I plan to present it may shock some of the students of these masters; but I am sure it would never surprise the masters themselves. For, though heavy stress has been laid on the incontrovertible truth that Mass is a communal act, an act that enfolds every member of the Mystical Body, and reaches out even to those who have never been incorporated into that Body, I will speak of Mass only as it affects the individual in the here and now.

This approach will be personal in two senses of the word: the subjective and the objective. I am speaking to my readers. I am speaking also to and of myself. I can tell my petitioners how to get more out of Mass only if I tell them how it is that I have come to get so much out of it. For thirty years now, Lord, You have allowed me to be Your lips as I bent above bread, Your voice as I bent over wine. For thirty years You have allowed me to be You, as I said: "This is My Body. This is My Blood." Now, after those thirty marvelous years, Lord, whenever I am asked to define Mass, I depart from the official wording of Trent. I never use the text of any catechism. Strictly speaking, I do not define; I describe. But I know that description makes Mass alive for me, I feel certain it can make Mass live for all others. To any man, woman, or even child, who wants to know what Mass is, I say: *O admirabile commercium* — "A wondrous exchange!" To every man, woman, and child who wants to "get more out of Mass,"

I now say: Make Mass what Christ wanted Mass to be when He said: "Do this in memory of me." Make Mass that *admirabile commercium* — "that wondrous exchange" in which God gives Himself to you and you give yourself to God.

You well know, Lord, how I live with that *Introibo ad altare Dei* — "I will go unto the altar of God" — as the focal point of my day. You know Your altar is the center of my life and of all my living; that wheat and wine symbolize the universe for me. You know how it is with me when I am privileged to celebrate three Masses in succession as on All Souls' Day and on Christmas: I am loathe to leave the altar; I would gladly go on again and again with this Act of Love, making this "wondrous exchange" endlessly. And You well know just when and how Mass came to be my life. It was at that blessed moment when I suddenly realized that Mass was not something but *Someone* — that it was YOU! It was then that I knew I held in my hands the Victim of Calvary, true, but as Victor more than as Victim; the slain Lamb of God, yes, but as living now and never to die again. Once it came home to me that it is the glorified Lord who comes under the appearances of bread and wine, I knew that we are in glory during the celebration of Mass much more than on Golgotha. That truth changes life, makes the world different, and time an incalculably precious treasure. Thanks to this truth I saw what Mass is, was, and ever will be an act of love in which God is the Lover, who not only gives Himself for men, but to men — and awaits man's return of love in like totality. Then it was that I saw that the antiphon, *O admirabile commercium,* with which we Trappists greet each new day is Your love song, Lord, and ours; and is a perfect description of Mass.

It has been said that love laughs at definition. That may be so. But, surely, anyone who has ever really loved will never question the perfection of this antiphon as a description of love. We monks sing it in its entirety every morning. It is a beautiful thing, Lord. It loses some of its lilt in translation, but none of its beauty, love, or truth. "O wondrous exchange: the Creator of the human race taking to Himself a living body, deigned to be born of a virgin, and coming forth a man without the concurrence of man, bestows on us men His divinity." That, dear Lord, is love — for it is You! And that, dear Lord, is exactly what everyone should see when he looks at Mass.

You know I am asking Your indulgence to depart a bit from the usual presentation of Mass, Lord. And You know why I ask it. Of course every Mass is of, by, and for the entire Mystical Body, and even for the whole human race. But, since the whole is the sum of its *parts,* and a body is made up of its *members,* what Paul said of himself, every human being can say of his own self in relation to You and Your Act of Love called Mass: *Dilexit me, et tradidit semetipsum pro me* — "He loved *me,* and gave himself up for *me*" (Gal 2:20). Love is personal, Lord. So is Mass; for Mass is Love. Hence I am going to present it as personal.

As I see it, Lord, the question put by these good people is not only vitally important and personal, but is personally vital and of eternal import. For one may as well look for sunshine without any sun, sea-foam without any sea, or a lily's bloom without ever a lily's bulb, as to look for holiness apart from Holiness's Font: You and Your Mass. So let me now show them how "to get more out of Mass" as well as how to put more into Mass, by showing them that Mass is not something but *Someone* — that it is You in Your greatest Act of Love; that it is You acting out this "wondrous exchange" in which You not only take our humanity, but give us of Your divinity. In short, Lord, let us teach them that *THIS IS LOVE.*

PART ONE

GOD IS IN YOUR HANDS

CHAPTER ONE

LOVE AND HOLINESS

What it means to be "in Christ Jesus"

1

What is in your mind as you set out for Mass?

I asked that question of a Catholic college senior recently and received the honest but very disconcerting reply: "O Lord, how I hate to leave my bed."

Were you to be as honest, would your reply be as disconcerting?

I grieve for any human being who thinks such thoughts as he sets out for what is, in literal truth, the greatest event possible on earth. But I grieve even more for the great, good, all-holy God who made such an event possible not only every day in the week, but every hour of the day, and every second of each hour, somewhere in this world. This heart-bursting generosity on the part of God, this beggaring of Himself in His all-out love, should be winning from man an appreciation that would so revolutionize lives as to re-create our universe.

If Christ was forced, as it were, to say to the woman at Jacob's well with whom He had had but a few words: "If you understood God's gift and knew who he is that speaks to you . . ." what can He not say to us who should understand and who should know that in Mass He not only speaks to us, but gives us God's Only Word — Himself?

What would your existence be like had Christ at His Last Supper decreed that only once in your lifetime could a priest do what He had done there in the Cenacle? Or to make it more concrete, suppose that on that same momentous night, this same Jesus Christ had decided that Mass should be offered only once every fifty years, and then only at Gethsemani, Kentucky. How would you spend your years, your days, all your hours? Would not this monastery become the focal point of your universe? Would not your days, weeks, months, all your years be spent preparing for that one morning when you could come here and meet your God in an intimacy that baffles description? What would your life be like if you saw so deeply into this Mystery that you came to the realization that it is admirably described in the antiphon about that "wondrous exchange"; that not only is bread and wine transubstantiated, but that you can be transformed, as you are made to live with the very life of God and are assimilated, as it were, more and more into the Divinity?

Faced with such a supposition, we are forced to admit that we do not appreciate God and His goodness. We do not realize that Mass is not only alive with God but is meant to set us alive with the same life. Why is it that we have not come to this appreciation and realization? The answer is simple: we do not reflect sufficiently; we do not probe; we are too easily satisfied with what lies on the surface. Let us be honest: We have not understood this "gift of God."

None of us likes to make such an admission, but facts are stubborn things; and that this is fact can be rather easily demonstrated by taking as illustration first that which occurs about eighteen times a year in the city of Naples. On the various feasts connected with St. Januarius, the principal patron of that city, a small glass phial half filled with a black, opaque substance, believed to be the blood of that martyr, is taken by a priest and held close to what is reputed to be the head of that martyr. The people, who crowd the church on every such occasion, pray, and pray earnestly. After some time, varying from two minutes to an hour, the dark mass, hitherto solid and immovable, detaches itself from the sides of the glass, becomes liquid, turns reddish in color, bubbles as if boiling, and increases in volume. When this occurs the priest announces: "The miracle has happened," and immediately that church is set ringing with cries of exultation. The *Te Deum* is then intoned and the excited assembly takes it up with gusto.

Records of this happening go back over four hundred years. Few, if any, alleged miracles have been examined more carefully, more often, or by people of more divergent views than this liquefaction of the blood of St. Januarius. Consequently, today no one, no matter how rationalistic in temper, can deny that what is said to take place *does* take place. It is an awe-filling event. No one can question that. But what is the liquefaction of mere human blood compared to what takes place in every Mass? When any priest turns to the faithful, holds up the transubstantiated Host, and says: *Ecce Agnus Dei,* — "Behold the Lamb of God" — he is speaking factually. He is telling you to look and see the very same Person the Jews looked upon that first Good Friday morning when the harassed Roman governor, Pontius Pilate, said to them: *Ecce homo* — and pointed to Jesus Christ. In literal truth it is the same Jesus Christ, but He is now in a far different condition. Then He was bloody, beaten, a horror to behold. Now He is radiant with glory, as resplendent as ever He was at the Transfiguration. Yet, what is your reaction, or that of the rest of the faithful at Mass? Compare it with that shown by the faithful at Naples when the priest announces that "the miracle has happened"; then ask yourself: "How superficial can we be?"

Or take what happens in Rome whenever a jubilee year is proclaimed. From every corner of the globe come pilgrims, many of whom have saved for a lifetime just to make this one trip possible. But for what? — A plenary indulgence. Now no one is questioning the value of such an indulgence. It is what it is called: plenary. It takes away all the temporal punishment due to one's sins, no matter how heinous they may have been, nor how numerous. This is marvelous mercy on the part of God. But what is it compared to what transpires in every Mass and is actualized in every Holy Communion? At Rome the indulgence is possible. Whether one gains it or not will never be known this side of eternity. In Mass Christ is actual. He, the Son of God, and very God, is present to take away not only the temporal punishment due to the sins of one individual, but as the priest always says: *Qui tollit peccata mundi* — "Who takes away the sins of the world." Furthermore, He is there just as He is in heaven — *semper vivens* — "alive"! It is the living God, and the God of all the living, who is in every Mass; and there for the set purpose Paul spoke of: *ad interpellandum pro nobis* — "to intercede for us." But more. He is there for something much more personal, much more intimate, much more vital. He is there to love and be loved. He is there to give Himself to us and take us to Himself. He is there for that "wondrous exchange" which He will make as only God could make it: by giving Himself to us as Food and Drink, and taking us to Himself by having this same Food and Drink assimilate us to Him, rather than we assimilating It to us. Mass is that *sacrum convivium* St. Thomas Aquinas told about: that holy living together in a divinely hallowing manner; for in Mass Christ is not only the Living Bread, but also the Life-giving Bread: Aquinas was exact: *vitam praestans homini* — Christ gives life to man; His own Divine Life, in and through Mass.

And yet, what are our thoughts as we set out for Mass?

Is not one forced to wonder if we would not be much more highly appreciative of God's generosity if He had not been so generous? Just think again on that supposition about Mass being offered once in your lifetime, and then only here at Gethsemani. Would not your life have a center, you a very definite goal, and every passing hour a very specific meaning? You would be awaiting that one definite moment when you could meet your loving God in person, not only to pay Him homage as His creature, but to love Him and be loved by Him as His child. More than likely Mass would then be for you what Mass was meant to be when Christ said: "Do this as my memorial" (Lk 22:19). It would be *agape* — a "love feast."

Had I asked that college senior what his thoughts were as he set out to meet his girl friend, do you think I would have heard anything about sleep? He would not only be awake, he would be fully alive. His heart would know no sluggish beat, nor his feet any slow, heavy step. This would be true if he was only attracted to the girl; doubly true if he was infatuated with her; and practically an understatement if he was actually in love with her. For he would be on his way to meet a person — someone with whom there could be an "exchange"; someone to whom he could give, and from whom he could receive, that which we call love. He would be setting out to meet a person whose presence could affect his entire being.

The word "person" has been heavily stressed because the too little recognized fact is that love can exist only between persons. We hear people say they love a dog, a horse, a cat, a flower; that they love a song, a tree, a book. What they are uttering is actual nonsense. For love can exist only between persons. It demands that one person gives to another person. If it is real love, the person receiving the gift of love will make a return of love to the person giving. Love is an "exchange." When found in its fullness it is seen to be an exchange between persons of their very selves. This is true in marriage. It is even more true in Mass.

Consequently, the dominant thought as you set out for Mass should be: I am going to meet a Person. This Person means life to me. In literal truth, He is my life; for He is my God and my all. He is my Lover. I am on my way to meet One who has loved me before the heavens ever knew a sun, or the night sky any stars; for He has loved me "with an everlasting love" (Jer 31:3). Yes, and He has loved me "to death — even to death on a cross" (Phil 2:8). He has loved me as no man or woman can love me; for He is divine. I am on my way to hold rendezvous with my God; to have a tryst with One who can transform me, who longs to make me better than I am, and who can make His longing come true. I am on my way to meet my living, loving God who actually yearns for me with a living love infinitely greater than even a mother can harbor in her wondrously loving heart.

That is reality. Were we as realistic as we so often think we are, would not time seem to stop for us, and space dissolve, and all things cease to be, as we hurried to this rendezvous with Him who is Love by essence, and who longs to make us more and more like Himself?

I remember hearing how a priest at his golden jubilee of ordination held his audience spellbound as he told them how his attitude toward Mass had gradually changed with the years. He confessed what every newly ordained, most likely, has to confess: how the night before his first Mass was not night at all. He could hardly sleep; the hours moved on with dragging, leaden feet. Then with dawn came that surge of holy expectation; that tingling to the fingertips; that craving of the whole being to get to the altar and hold Christ in his hands. Mass that morning, and for many a morning after, was filled to the overflowing with spiritual joy. The Cenacle, Calvary, Heaven itself seemed near; nearer than earth; closer than the altar. Christ, too, was real — alive! The consecrated Host seemed almost to palpitate. But now, as golden jubilarian, far from impatience with time, and that excited eagerness to get to the altar, he knew only a holy hesitancy, almost a holy dread. "For now," he said, "I realize that I am holding in my hands *the living God.*"

At first you may be taken by this confession, and admire the man for his keen realization of the majesty of God, and the infinite distance there is, and ever will be, between Creator and creature. You may even be tempted to applaud his recognition of the transcendence of Him who is God, and the consequent consciousness of the unworthiness of the human being to be in the presence of the Divine. But I beg you not to yield to that temptation until we have thought this through, and have come to a true realization of the guise under which we meet God in Mass.

It is the Holy Trinity's Second Person whom you meet in Mass. He is divine. He is "God of God, true God of true God," as we sing in the *Credo* of the Mass. But He is not there as Omnipotence, though His omnipotence is truly there. Hence, you need never shrink before His power when Mass is being offered; for Almighty God is not there as The Almighty. Nor need you cringe before

His infinite majesty, though that majesty is there in all its infinite-
ness. Nor is there any call for that fear which one may feel in the
presence of a judge who is to pass a sentence from which there is
no appeal. Christ, who is Mass, will one day be our Judge; but
He does not come as Judge in Mass; He comes only in one guise —
that of a Lover.

You meet God in Mass. Never forget that. You meet Him in
Person, but garbed in that personality, if you will allow the word,
of the Good Samaritan, the Good Shepherd, or the Father of the
Prodigal. Actually, it is in the personality of the One who, with
His dying gaze, looked upon those who had just driven spikes
through His hands and feet to affix Him to that awful cross, that
gibbet of shame, then lifted His voice in prayerful plea to His
Father, asking Him to "forgive them," saying that "they do not
know what they are doing" (Lk 23:34). That is the personality
in which you meet God in Mass. It is that of Him who looked with
almost His last glance upon a thief who was dying with Him and
said: "I assure you, this very day you will be with me in paradise"
(Lk 23:43). It cannot be overstressed that you meet God in Mass,
but it must not be understressed that you meet Him as the One who
would not condemn the woman taken in adultery, forgave the
Magdalene, stated bluntly that He had "come for sinners," and
summed up His mission in the words: "I have come that they may
have life and have it in abundance" (Jn 10:10).

Since that is the guise in which God is met in Mass, you will
understand why this aging priest, your present instructor, far from
experiencing any lessening of that holy impatience he knew before
his first Mass, that sleep-forbidding longing to be vested and to
stand holding Him in his hands, knows now an ever greater concentration of time. My day seems all of one hour — the hour of Mass.
Every moment leads to my meeting with my God — or away from
today's meeting and on toward tomorrow's. God is my life. I have
Him in Mass in the most tangible form possible this side of eternity.
Small wonder, then, that Mass is my life!

As for you — realize that in Mass you meet God not as your

Maker, certainly not as your Judge, in one sense not even as your Redeemer, but only as your Lover. For this is He who said: "I have loved thee with an everlasting love" (Jer 31:3); who can say again today what He said in the long, long ago, and have it be even more spectacularly true; namely, "Can a woman forget her infant, so as not to have pity on the child of her womb? And if she should forget, yet will not I forget thee. Behold, I have graven thee in my hands" (Is 49:15)? Yes, in those hands which hold Calvary's nail prints, but which now glow like suns. Here is He who repeats by His love-radiating presence what He once put into words in the parables of Solomon: "My child, give me thy heart" (Prv 23:26). You meet Him as that One who said, and still says: "O come to me all you who are weary and overburdened, and I will refresh you" (Mt 11:28). That is the God you are to meet, and that is the guise in which you are to see Him. He who once "loved you to death" is waiting in every Mass to love you to life.

Do you believe in love at first sight? Some have doubted it; many still dispute it; some even deny it. My own opinion on the matter is not really relevant here; but what is relevant and what I am absolutely certain of is this: there can be no love at all unless there is first some kind of sight. The Scholastics have an axiom on it which runs: *Nihil amatum nisi praecognitum,* which means that you cannot love someone you do not know. But you cannot know anyone you have never seen in some way or other. So the axiom stands. Like every other axiom this one holds common sense; for it is derived from common experience. But you can go further than that. You can say that this truth is based not only on the universal experience of men, but on the public revelation of God; for, in his very first Epistle, John, the Beloved Disciple, wrote: "He who does not love his brother whom he sees, cannot love God whom he does not see" (1 Jn 4:20). Those words could never have been inspired by God the Holy Spirit if sight of some sort was not an absolute necessity before one can love with any reality. We simply must rest our eyes on "the object of our affection" — if not the eyes of the body, then most certainly those of the soul. Hence, if

Mass is to be what Mass is meant to be, and if you are to get out of it all you should, you simply must *see* God in it. You must stand face to face with Jesus Christ — see Him and be seen by Him. There is no other possibility; for Mass is an Act of Love, and love's first requisite as well as its first intimacy is *sight*.

"I am going to see God!" That is one thought which should be uppermost in your mind as you set out for Mass. You are going to see Him, hold tryst with Him, meet Him as Lover. Like every true lover He will take you to Himself to make you better, more like Himself. He will transform you through His loving, make you holy with His own holiness, and thus make you presentable to, and acceptable by, God the Father. Thus will His Mass become that "wondrous exchange." In literal truth it will be *sacrum facere* — "a making holy" — from which our word "sacrifice" is derived.

With those truths before you, you are in position to see why Mass must be your life, and your life a Mass. For the glorious ultimate of your life and all your living is to be made so holy with God's own holiness, that you will be not only presentable to, but acceptable by, God — in time as well as for eternity. Mass is the well-spring whence comes this Living Water, for Mass is the fountainhead of all holy living, since it is Jesus Christ who is living Holiness. Of Him we sing in Mass: *Tu solus sanctus* — "Thou alone art holy"; but you are His member in that Body of which He is the Head.

2

This being so, you can see how right our university professor was when he sought to become holy through Mass. Strictly speaking, there is no other source. Nor has life any other meaning. You and I were made to be holy with the holiness of God. Fail that, and we have failed to live. God gave us holiness as our vocation, as our only career, as the one lasting achievement of our earthly existence. That is the challenge, the adventure, the romance meant for each of us who has sprung from Adam and Eve, and been resprung from Jesus Christ. Consequently, it is "in Christ Jesus" alone that we can live, move, and have any real being; and again we say: He is Mass.

It was this same university professor who challenged me to tell him just what it meant to be "in Christ Jesus." No wonder he got so little out of Mass; for what can Mass mean to any of us unless we realize clearly that we *are* "in Christ Jesus."

God, the Holy Spirit, made this stupendous gift of God intelligible by using three figures which are as tangible as your fingers. The first is that of a stone. Just at present, we, here in Gethsemani, are renewing our monastery. In our yard, stones have lain for weeks. Yesterday, some were lifted to the third floor and installed as sills for the new windows. Now, to use a word that is a favorite among the moderns, those stones are functional. They are serving a purpose they could never have served so long as they lay in the yard. Before they could have been said to have any practical value, they had to become part of the monastic building. Before yesterday these stones were simply isolated bits of rock laying about. Now they are closely related to every other stone in the building, and together with them form an edifice that means much to us monks and, consequently, much to God. St. Peter, the first Pope, speaking to the earliest Christians, told them that "as living stones" they were "being built into a spiritual edifice, so as to be a holy priesthood to offer up spiritual sacrifices which will be acceptable to God through Jesus Christ" (1 Pt 2:5).

Just as the stones that were made into sills became integral parts of our monastery, so Christians are integrated into Christ whom Peter calls the "living stone" and named as our "cornerstone." We who are "in Christ Jesus" are parts of that "spiritual edifice" wherein "acceptable sacrifices are offered to God." We have been made one with Jesus Christ just as truly as those stones have been made one with our monastery. The analogy is a good one, but Peter did have to stretch his figure a bit by speaking of "living stones." Paul was more fortunate in his choice of figures. He gave us two which will illustrate the phrase "in Christ Jesus" with much greater clarity for most of us.

First — that of a graft. In his letter to the Romans, Paul, speaking to the Gentiles, likened Israel, the Chosen People of God, to an olive tree. He admits that some of the branches have been broken off, and says that the Gentiles, like a "wild olive," have been grafted in their place, and thus made to partake "of the root and the richness of the olive tree" (Rom 11:17). Christ, of course, is the "root and richness," and Paul very pointedly insisted that the Gentiles "remember that it is not you who support the root, but the root that supports you." What a vivid illustration that is for any who have seen a graft or made one. The life of the tree into which the graft is inserted rises from the root, goes into that graft, and not only enlivens it, but transforms it so that it becomes a living part of that living tree. So with us Christians, who, by Baptism, have been grafted into Christ Jesus. We live with His life. We become living parts of His Living Self.

The Apostle uses figurative language to describe the reality, but the reality he describes is anything but figurative. We are "in Christ Jesus." Instead of that of a grafted branch, a more telling illustration might be that of the root reaching out into the soil, taking up lifeless minerals, transforming them into living matter, thus elevating them to an existence they could never have known had not the roots taken hold of them. Jesus Christ is the "Root of Jesse." Through His Sacrament of Baptism, He reaches out and takes us, who were as lifeless as minerals in the soil as far as the God-life is concerned, transforms us, elevates us as He sets us living with His own Divine Life. That is what it means to be "in Christ Jesus."

The best known illustration, of course, is that given by St. Paul in many different Epistles — that of the Body. He wrote: ". . . just as the body is a unit, although it has many members, and all the members of the body, many though they are, form but one body, so too is the Christ. In fact, by a single Spirit all of us, whether Jews or Greeks, slaves or freemen, were introduced into the one body through baptism. . . . You are Christ's body, and individually its members" (1 Cor 12:12–14, 27).

Surely that illustration makes all quite clear; for each of us has a body made up of many members, and we not only say that each member is ours, but in some way each member is us; for it lives by our life, and we live in it. "So, too, is the Christ." Or as Paul put it when writing to his Galatians: "It is now no longer I who live, but Christ lives in me" (Gal 2:20).

But even better than the illustrations given by Peter and Paul, I like the one given by Christ Himself. On the very night He instituted Mass, Christ gave us what is, if not the clearest, then surely the most unforgettable of illustrations. "I am the vine," He said, "you are the branches. One bears abundant fruit only when he and I are mutually united; severed from me, you can do nothing. If one does not remain united with me, he is simply thrown away like a branch, and dries up. . . . This is what glorifies my Father — your bearing abundant fruit" (Jn 15:5–8).

You know why the severed vine branch dries up: it has not the life of the vine in it. What a lesson for life, and a lesson in real living that gives us Christians. If we will live, we must cling to the Vine. If we would live fruitful lives, we must have the holiness of Christ coursing through our veins as really as branches have the sap of the vine coursing through theirs. We must live "in Christ Jesus" — and be "alive to God" with the very life of Jesus Christ. Where can we do this more surely than in Mass where we meet Him who "alone is holy" and meet Him as that Lover who would give us His love in the form of life?

The ways of God have been called "inscrutable." Unquestionably, in many things, they are. But in this matter of holiness for the people of God there is a unity in revelation that makes for a crystal clarity. For we read in Leviticus how God spoke to Moses and, through him, to the people he was leading toward the Promised Land. He said: "Be holy, for I am holy . . ." (Lv 11:44). That command came only after a choice on the part of God of this people to be His people, and the making of a covenant with them. "If you will obey my voice and keep my covenant, you shall be my own possession," said the Lord, "and you shall be a kingdom of priests and a holy nation." The people accepted that covenant: "All that the Lord has spoken we will do," they said (Ex 19:5–8).

That same command and, practically speaking, that same covenant we find again in the New Testament; for, in what can be called the first of all papal encyclicals, Peter wrote: "As he who has called you is holy, be holy yourselves in all your conduct; since it is written: 'You shall be holy, for I am holy' " (1 Pt 1:16). Then this first Pope gave the illustration already mentioned as he exhorted the first Christians to "Come to him, the Living Stone . . . and like living stones be yourselves built into a spiritual house, to be a holy priesthood . . . you are a chosen race, a royal priesthood, a holy nation, God's own people" (1 Pt 2:4–9). Then he pointed to the Source of this holiness and that priesthood by pointing to Christ and telling of His Mass, saying: "He bore our sins in his body on the cross that we, having died to sin, might live for holiness. By his wounds you were healed" (1 Pt 2:24).

Peter was quite explicit. But Paul was more emphatic. Almost every one of his Epistles opens with some reminder that his readers have been called by God "in Christ Jesus" to holiness; and that it is only "in Christ Jesus" that they can ever answer that call. The Romans, Corinthians, Galatians, Ephesians, Philippians, Colossians, and Thessalonians all read how "before the foundation of the world" they had been "chosen by God in Christ Jesus" to become holy, that in Him and through Him they were called to be saints.

What Moses announced to the Jews of old, what Peter and Paul proclaimed to the early Christians, has been made known to us of the twentieth century by every vicar of Christ of this century. They were but making known to us that one plan of God which was conceived "before the foundation of the world": namely, "to gather all creation both in heaven and on earth under one head, Christ" (Eph 1:10) — "the Holy One of God." Hence, we have heard the command of God: "Be ye holy, for I am holy."

That is the command which makes Mass as important to us as the breath we breathe, the blood that courses through our veins, the soul that animates our bodies; for through Mass, in Mass, by Mass we become holy with the holiness of God.

But one must realize if he would be genuinely holy, he must be brave, very brave. For he must not only not be afraid of fire, but must actually crave to be burned. There is no other way. For our God is Fire.

It was with rare insight that Cardinal Newman once made his prayer for holiness by turning to Christ and saying: "Flood my soul with Thy Spirit and life; penetrate and possess my whole being so utterly that all my life may be but a radiance of Thine; shine through me and be so in me that every soul I come in contact with may feel Thy Presence in my soul; let them look up and see no longer me — but only Jesus! Stay with me and then I shall begin to shine as Thou shinest, so to shine as to be a light to others; the light, O Jesus, will be all from Thee, and none of it from me; it will be Thou shining on others through me."

That gives you a very excellent idea of what holiness is; for, to be exact, our holiness consists in a loving union with God through and in Jesus Christ. Therefore, true Christian living is steady contact with the Divine, a conscious constant cultivation of intimacy with the Infinite; literally, it means that we enter into the universe of God's own holiness. Hence the need for bravery; for the holiness of God is flame — the living flame of Love.

It is said that "the burned child dreads the fire." That can never be true about the child of God and his attitude toward the fire of holiness. Look at Moses. He met God. At first it was as fire. A burning bush attracted his attention. He approached it to ascertain how it was that it burned and yet was not consumed. As he neared it he was told to "put off his shoes, for he was on holy ground." What made the ground holy? The presence of the all-holy God — the God of Abraham, Isaac, and Jacob (cf. Ex 3:4 ff.). God was in that fire which "burned but did not consume"; but that fire was not God. Yet we are told in Deuteronomy that our God *"is* a consuming fire" (4:22) and by Him we must be set ablaze before we are holy with the holiness He has called us to, and which His

Son has made possible for us to achieve through and in His Mass.

On Sinai Moses again met God, and again it was in fire. It was in fire, too, that many of the prophets met God. Ezechiel, for instance, as he sat by the waters of the Chobar. A whirlwind swept down on him, but when he looked into the flaming heart of it he saw God. Even with that celebrated vision of Isaias there is fire. For when this Prophet saw "the Lord sitting upon a high throne and elevated: and his train filling the temple," he also saw the seraphim and heard their song of praise which tells the very nature of God: "Holy, Holy, Holy." He then bewailed his condition as one with unclean lips. But one of the seraphim flew to him with a live coal, which he had taken from the altar — and cleansed those lips. Before God, then, who is "a consuming Fire" and who is subsistent Holiness, there is an altar with fire upon it.

Fire is but one form under which the holiness of God is represented to us, yet it is perhaps, the most persistent form — in both Testaments. All that was prefigured in the Old Testament reaches climax and fulfillment when Jesus "the Flaming word of God" (Ps 17:31) comes. John the Baptist promised that the Christ of God would baptize with "the Holy Spirit and with Fire" (Lk 3:16). Christ Himself tells us that He has come "to cast fire" (Lk 12:49). What is this Fire but the Fire of Love and Holiness? He sends His Holy Spirit, the Spirit of Love, upon His Apostles; and He sends Him in the shape of "tongues of Fire" (Acts 2:3). And the last form in which we see Christ in the Apocalypse is as One from whose eyes the Spirit blazes out.

If we are to be holy, then, we must not only approach this God who is a consuming Fire, this Christ who came to cast Fire, this Spirit who fell as Flame, but we must somehow be transformed by Them into Them. That is Holiness, and nothing else is.

Of course we are speaking figuratively. But is there any other way to make this truth clear? Holiness is our vocation "in Christ Jesus." We must, therefore, be transformed into Him. So we take the figure of flame; for, of all nonliving elements, this is the one that most nearly lives. It does most of those things we associate with life: it moves, it assimilates, it transforms. It takes combustible matter and makes it "live" with its "life."

You have, of course, watched a flame taking hold of a log. It is a fascinating, almost a mesmerizing experience. The blue-gold, wavering loveliness of the flame will lick the sides of the log which may be dull gray and covered with an unsightly, scaly bark. There seems no affinity whatsoever between the two: the flame seems all life, loveliness, and ever active; the log seems utterly dead, unmoving, and almost unmovable. But as you watch, you will see a transformation take place. Soon little tongues of flame will be coming out of the log here and there. Then that blue-gold brilliance will grow and grow until it completely envelops the log. Finally, the log and the flame will be one: total transformation has been accomplished: the dead has come to life as it were; ugliness has taken on beauty; the inert and seemingly unmovable is now ever moving and gives forth magnificence as well as comfort and warmth.

That is something of a symbol of what takes place in man by the action of God who is Fire and Flame. That gives a very vivid idea of what it means to become holy. It means that we must be taken hold of by God, the All-Holy, changed by Him, transformed by Him, made over by Him, and this time made much more like unto Him.

How is this done? We were not born holy. We cannot make ourselves holy. Yet holy we must become or fail in the real purpose of our existence. Mass is the answer; the only answer. For Mass is Christ, and He alone is holy. But before that reply will really register with us, we will have to review a few fundamental truths. First of all: God made us. Second, being an all-wise God, He had a purpose for making us. Being a provident God He had a plan according to which we were supposed to attain that purpose.

I would apologize for presenting such basic facts were there not other facts almost staring us out of countenance, thus compelling us to belabor what to many will seem obvious. Here are some of those facts. . . .

Insecurity is the hallmark of the modern. Why is he so insecure? Do not point to atomic fission, nor to the almost magical IBM's. Do not cite the latest menacing line of the Reds. These things might make for insecurity if men were machines or if we had here a "lasting city." But how can there be any insecurity in the life of one who knows he was made by God and for God; that he. "has not here a lasting city, but looks for one that is to come"; that life is a wind, and eternity, tomorrow? How can there be any insecurity for one who has a detailed map of life; a map which is in relief, clearly showing the terrain he must traverse, and even marking out in red the safe, sure road he must take to arrive at his destination in safety and with assurance?

Yet, there is insecurity all around us. You see it in life, in literature, on the stage and screen. The very atmosphere seems saturated with anxiety, unrest, paralyzing fear. But there is no need for any of this. All modern man — be he young, middle-aged, or old — has to do is look to Christ and His Mass. He is the Way. Those who are "in Him" meet the destructive fire of bombs with the constructive fire of Love; the depersonalization of Cybernetics by assuming the character and "personality" of the Holy Trinity's Second Person; meet the transiency of earth and all things earthly by the eternality of grace and of God. They have everything "in Christ Jesus." But they must "put Him on." They must, in other words, become holy with the holiness of God — and they can do it in, through, and by Mass.

What every man needs is a fundamental principle that will integrate life and give meaning to all living. That principle is not hard to find. Actually, we could follow the deepest dynamism of our hearts — and be safe. But we need not; for God, who put that dynamism into our beings, has clarified, specified, particularized the way this drive should function, not by giving us a detailed plan to follow, but by giving us a Person to love and become like. Christ came to earth for one set purpose: to make that Act of Love we call Mass. We Christians are on earth for no other ultimate purpose. Our lives must be an Act of Love like

unto Christ's — an Act of Love for God. That Act we can make
perfectly in Mass; for, as the end of the Canon so beautifully
expresses it, it is here that "through, with, and in Christ Jesus we
give God all honor and glory."

The glory of God is why Christ came. The glory of God is why
you and I exist. We were brought into being, and have been kept
in being for one ultimate purpose: to give glory to God. That is
the first, fundamental, and final purpose of our lives and all our
living. That is true whether we live those lives in time or in eternity.
In eternity, however, there will be no difficulty about our functioning properly: we will give glory to God faultlessly as His saints,
or He will take it from us as He does from the angels who fell and
were condemned. But so long as we are in time, there will always
be danger, and always difficulty about our rendering God what is
His due by being what we are created to be. That is why it is
imperiously important to be "in Christ Jesus."

At the end of each psalm, hymn, and prayer in choir, we monks
bend over in adoration and sing a doxology: we praise God the
Father, God the Son, and God the Holy Spirit. We give glory to
each Person of the Holy Trinity. For me, and for most other
monks, this chant not only epitomizes the entire canonical Office,
but specifies the purpose of monasticism, and of each individual
monk. I could not count the times, after singing *Gloria Patri, et
Filio, et Spiritui Sancto* . . . I have risen from my adoring posture
saying to myself: "This is really fulfilling the purpose of existence.
This is life. This is true living. This is why God brought me into
being — to be a living, breathing doxology."

I was right to an extent; but not completely so. True it is that
we have been created by God to be animated doxologies. But it is
not in and through choir that we become such in all reality, but
only in and through Christ; and while it is true that the day's
Divine Office is directed toward the day's Mass, it is only in Mass
that we become what we have been made to be. For in Mass we
are taken most fully into Him who is the *Splendor Paternae Gloriae*
— "Splendor of the Father's Glory" — and can say with special

meaning *per Ipsum, et cum Ipso, et in Ipso* (we can stress that *in Ipso*) *est Tibi Deo Patri Omnipotenti, in unitate Spiritus Sancti, omnis honor et gloria.*

How Mass clarifies life and specifies the nature of the holiness we must acquire while living on earth! Too often we think of holiness in terms of morality. He or she is considered a holy person if he or she is known to keep the Commandments of God. We look upon the Decalogue as a font of holiness. It is not. The Decalogue would never make any of us into those "animated doxologies" which is the ultimate of our lives. Morality is an effect, not a cause of holiness. For, as we have come to realize, holiness is an ontological quality given us by Him who is supremely holy, uniquely holy, absolutely and essentially holy, completely other from us, to whom, nevertheless, He grants a share in his holiness, and makes us, as St. Peter says: "partakers of the Divine nature" (2 Pt 1:4). It was Christ who won this grant for us, and won it by His Mass; and nowhere are we more "in Christ Jesus" than we are in Mass.

We were placed "in Christ Jesus" by Baptism. That wondrous Sacrament marked our birth. But it is not enough to be born; one must grow. Just as a human infant must grow and grow in order to become a man, so we Christians must grow and grow in order to become *Christ*. That is the exalted and exalting reality of our existence. How frightening, and utterly frustrating it would be had not Christ, on the fourteenth day of the month Nisan, said to His Apostles: "Do this as my memorial" (Lk 22:19). With those words He gave us the means to become more and more Christ. Were more meaningful words ever spoken?

One day, in one of our eastern cities, a street reporter pushed a microphone before a young man who was passing by and asked him: "What do you consider the most important words ever spoken by any man on earth?" For the best part of an hour this reporter had been putting this same question to passersby. Varied indeed were the responses he had received. But little did he, or anyone listening in, expect the profound reply that was now given. The young man, who was not identified, took one look at the reporter, gave a quick glance at the "mike," and without a moment's hesitation said: "This is My Body. This is My Blood" — and passed on.

Phenomenal reply, wasn't it? What "instantaneous presence of mind" that young man had. Yet, as you ponder the purpose of life and the meaning of your individual existence, you may slowly come to suspect that, as far as you are concerned, Christ spoke other words that are personally more meaningful to you than those wondrous words that effected the first transubstantiation of bread and wine into His Body and Blood. For how would you ever become holy with the holiness of God; how would you ever worship with an act worthy of your God; how would you ever be able to offer yourself as an "acceptable sacrifice" to God, had Christ not that same evening and at that same meal gone on to say: "Do this as my memorial"? Had Christ not made Mass possible for us we could never answer that plea St. Paul put to his Corinthians: "We entreat you, in Christ's name, make your peace with God. Christ never knew sin, and God made him into sin for us, so that in him we might be turned into the holiness of God" (2 Cor 5:15). Where are we more "in Him" than in Mass?

With that before you, you should appreciate why Bossuet once said: "There is nothing in the universe greater than Jesus Christ; and nothing in Jesus Christ greater than His Sacrifice; and nothing in His Sacrifice greater than that last sigh and precious moment which separated His all-adorable soul from His all-adorable body." That was this eloquent French Bishop's rhetorical description of Christ's Mass. Undoubtedly he had in mind what theology teaches as the essence of Mass: the double consecration, which so dramatically symbolizes the death of Christ. And his description is excellent. But while we thank God for undergoing death for us, we must thank Him even more for reuniting that all-adorable soul with that all-adorable body, and making that "precious moment" so well described by Bossuet, unending, even as it is rendered, in its re-presentation, differently.

Christ did all that by rising from the dead. He did it also by saying to His Apostles, and through them to their successors: "Do this as my memorial." For with those words He instituted both the Christian Priesthood and the Christian Sacrifice, without which this wondrous world of ours would indeed be a "vale of tears," you and I naught but wanderers in a land without water, and all our accomplishments, no matter how stupendous, naught but ashes for the wind. For while Blaise Pascal was right when he said, "Outside Jesus Christ we do not know what life is, nor death, nor God, nor ourselves," he would have been more right had he said: "Unless you are 'in Christ Jesus' you neither live, nor die, find God, or become yourself."

The men of our day are making fabulous discoveries, achieving goals once thought to be only the stuff dreams are made of, conquering realms deemed beyond all human reach. Yet, what are all their accomplishments, achievements, inventions, and discoveries compared to what you can do by fulfilling that command of Christ, as far as in you lies: "Do this as my memorial"?

The late John XXIII in his short reign as pope managed to change the whole atmosphere of Christendom, filling it with an eirenicism that promises well for the ecumenism he so dexterously encouraged. Barriers that had stood for centuries, and were thought by many to be impregnable, he broke down. Unquestionably, in this century of outstanding pontiffs, he turned out to be among the most outstanding. And yet, had he succeeded not only in re-uniting Christendom, but in converting the world to Christ; had he been suddenly endowed by God with power enough to implement every section of his masterly encyclical *Pacem in Terris* and bring true peace with justice to our embattled world, banishing forever the nuclear threat — likened by many to the Sword of Damocles, which we know hangs by a thread that seems to grow thinner and thinner; had he been enabled to have nations do away with their stockpiles of bombs and actually disarm, all that would have been as nothing compared to what he did every morning in the privacy of the papal chapel as he vested practically as every simple priest vests, and said what every simple priest says the world over: *Introibo ad altare Dei* — "I will go unto the altar of God" — and offered Mass.

That is not rhetoric. That is reality. Hence you may well ask what would you have been, what could you have become, without Christ — and His Mass.

The thirteenth chapter of the First Epistle to the Corinthians is known as the Hymn to Love. It is one of the most beautiful passages in all Scripture. It has been quoted again and again, and will go on being quoted again and again. But to bring this opening chapter to sharpest focus for you, to give you clearest realization of just what Mass is, and what it means to you, we will change the word "love" in the lines of St. Paul and substitute for it the name of Him who is Love — and who is Mass — and have that famous chapter read:

> If I should speak the languages of men and angels, but am not in Christ Jesus, I am no more than a noisy gong and a clanging cymbal. And if I should have the gift of inspired utterance, and have the key to all secrets, and master the whole range of knowledge, and if I should have wonder-working confidence so as to be able to move mountains, but am not in Christ Jesus, I am nothing. And if I should distribute all I have bit by bit, and should yield my body to the flames, but am not in Christ Jesus, it profits me nothing.
>
> One in Christ Jesus is long-suffering, is kind, is not envious; one in Christ Jesus does not brag, is not conceited, is not ill-mannered; is not self-seeking; one in Christ Jesus is not irritable, takes no note of injury, is not glad when injustice triumphs, is glad when truth prevails. One in Christ Jesus is always ready to make allowances, to trust, to hope, to be patient.

Borrowing again from St. Paul, we take what he used as preface to that magnificent hymn in praise of love, and use it as climax to this pointed praise of Christ which so conclusively proves that, in very truth, He is our life, our way, our all. We say: "Be eager always to have the gift that is more precious than all the others."

We have just pointed out what that gift is: life "in Christ Jesus." You will never live in Him more fully, nor more fruitfully, than by living in Him conscious of His Priesthood, His Victimhood, His

Sacrifice. In other words, conscious of His Mass. For it is in Mass you meet Christ as Sacrifice, Sacrificer, and Sacrificing. It is in Mass, also, that you find yourself for what you are, and what you are ever to be: the Priest who offers, the Victim who is offered, and the Sacrifice that is being offered; for in Mass you are "in Christ Jesus" to be and to do as He is and does.

Heretofore you did not get all you should have out of Mass because, perhaps, you failed to realize that Mass is an Act of Love — God's and yours; that Mass is the *admirabile commercium* — "that wondrous exchange" — which changes all life; that in Mass God the Son places Himself in your hands to be offered to God the Father in the unity of God the Holy Spirit as perfect honor, praise, and glory, and you place yourself in the hands of God "in Christ Jesus" to be offered to the same Godhead for the same sublime purpose.

Heretofore you may not have become as holy through Mass as you should have become because, perhaps, you did not realize that holiness is a share in the very nature of God, which can be had only in and from Him who shared our nature, and became the Font of all holiness for men by becoming the Lamb of God offering His Mass, and making it possible for you to offer Him and yourself in that one, same Mass.

You will get more and more out of Mass, and become holier and holier through Mass, if you will try to be ever conscious of the truth that Mass is not something but Someone, and that you, as priest, have that Someone in your hands to be offered to God, even as you, as victim, place yourself in His hands to be offered "through Him, with Him, and in Him," that "God the Father in the unity of the Spirit might have all honor and glory."

It could well be that most of your trouble stems from the fact that you have never been conscious enough of your own priesthood.

CHAPTER TWO

YOU ARE A PRIEST . . .

" . . . forever, according to the order of Melchisedech."

Suppose I had stopped you any Sunday or holyday of obligation as you made your way toward church and asked you what you were about to do, what would you have answered? Would you have said anything about meeting God in Person — and personally? Anything about holding rendezvous with your Lover? Anything at all about making an Act of Love by engaging in that "wondrous exchange"?

More than likely your reply would have been negative. But from now on I hope that the reality of Mass will be so clear to you that you will have no other thoughts more uppermost in your mind, nor any other longings throbbing in your heart than that you are setting out to love and be loved; that you are hurrying on your way to meet One who will give Himself to you in that totality which real love alone knows, and to whom you can give yourself with like loving abandon.

If I had stopped you, and your reply took any of the usual forms, such as: "I am *going* to Mass" or "I am setting out to *hear* Mass" or "I am on my way to *attend* Mass" *or* "I am hurrying to church *to be present* at Mass," you have an answer to your original question as to why you do not get more out of Mass, and why you do not become holier through Mass. For each of those expressed intentions denotes passivity, and if there is one thing you should not be at Mass, it is passive. Christ's command was: "*Do* this . . ." He commanded action.

Of course you may want to object, and argue that Christ's command was addressed immediately to the Eleven in the Supper Room, and, through them, to their successors, the ordained priests of the Church. In other words, you may want to insist that only those men who have received the Sacrament of Holy Orders have been the recipients of this command of Christ, and have the power to "*Do* this . . ."

Your objection is unanswerable if you limit priesthood in the New Law to the power of *consecrating* bread and wine. But have you any warrant for so limiting the idea of priesthood? Not if you recall all we brought before you concerning the Chosen People of God and their being a "royal priesthood" and a "consecrated nation"; not if you recall what St. Peter said in that letter we called the first papal encyclical; not if you remember all St. Paul taught in his letters to the Romans and the Hebrews. From these inspired passages in Holy Scripture it is evident that all the "people of God" have some sort of a priesthood. You belong to the "people of God." Therefore . . .

It will mean much to you, and your attitude toward Mass, if you will look deeply into your office in the New Law and its function. I have dared title this chapter "You Are a Priest," and added the lines found in Psalm 109, "according to the order of Melchisedech." And lest that last name puzzle you, let it be said that Melchisedech was the king of Salem who offered bread and wine. Need the parallel be pointed further?

You are a priest. . . . Therefore, you set out for church every Sunday and holyday of obligation to fulfill your priestly function, to perform your priestly duty, to exercise your priestly privilege. You set out to *offer* Mass. That is the only proper reply to the question I supposedly proposed to you; for to offer Mass is proper to the priesthood. But if there is one thing a priest may not be while offering Mass, it is passive. A recognition of your role as priest can change forever your attitude, not only toward Mass, but toward all life. It will actually change your universe as it gives you, as center for your world, your being "in Christ Jesus."

Why is it that earnest pastors can describe their Sunday congregations as "bored"? That word has a shriek to it that sets my nerves on end. "Bored" when all but face to face with God? "Bored" while sitting in the Cenacle with Jesus Christ? "Bored" while standing with Mary and John beneath that cross on which the world's Redemption hangs? "Bored" while looking at "the Lamb" of the Apocalypse "standing as if slain"? "Bored" while listening to the "ancients" before the throne, and hearing the heavenly Liturgy? "Bored" while being loved to death — and to life — by God Himself? Yet one of the latest descriptions of a congregation runs: ". . . the children fidget, the young people talk, the men are waiting for the end, the women are looking at their neighbors' dresses; everyone is bored."

Pius XI gives index to the cause of this "boredom" when he speaks of the faithful adopting the attitude of "detached and silent spectators." The cure for that "boredom" is given by his successor, Pius XII, who writes: "It is therefore desirable that all the faithful should be aware that to *participate* in the Eucharistic Sacrifice is their *chief duty* and *supreme dignity*." Nor does this Pontiff leave you in the dark as to the manner in which you are to "participate." For he goes on to say: ". . . not in any inert and negligent fashion, giving way to distractions and daydreaming, but with such earnestness and concentration that they may be united as closely as possible with the High Priest . . . and together with Him . . . and through Him . . . and in union with Him, let them offer up themselves" (*Mediator Dei*, § 80).

Whence does this learned Pontiff derive his idea about your "chief duty and supreme dignity"? From the too unfamiliar fact that you were ordained priest of God by your Baptism. Yes, you, whether you be male or female, convert or cradle Catholic, married or single, religious or lay, old or young, educated or not, you are a priest of God; for deep into your immortal soul was stamped the "sacramental character" which shows forth, and will forever show forth, the sacerdotal features of the One Priest of the New Law — Jesus Christ.

Too often we think of Baptism only as that Sacrament which frees us from original sin and any personal sin we may have committed before Baptism. It does that, of course. But it does ever so much more. Nor is it enough to rest satisfied with the usual explanations given in catechisms about the effects of this marvelous Sacrament. For while they tell much, they could still tell more. Most will tell you about being reborn "of the water and the Holy Spirit," consequently, of being made children of God, heirs of heaven, coheirs with Jesus Christ. They will go on and speak of the infusion of sanctifying and sacramental grace, tell of the Theological and Moral Virtues that have been granted us. They may even dwell long on the fact that we are indwelt by the Three Divine Persons. But how seldom do they speak of our having been made priests? Yet this effect of Baptism has been recognized and taught as truth from the beginning.

You have already seen how Scripture is filled with this teaching; for both the Old and the New Testaments tell how God chose His people to be a "nation of priests." Now take a quick glance at tradition. The Vicars of Christ, from Peter to Pius XII, have repeated it again and again. Pope Leo I put it most succinctly when he said: "Baptism is the *ordination* of the laity" (Serm. IV). Today we seldom hear it called an "ordination"; but, more and more frequently, we do hear tell of the "priesthood of the laity." The phrase is not new. Far from it. St. Jerome, back in the fourth century, used it, and connected it with its source: Baptism. For in his Dialogue against the Luceferians he talks of "the priesthood of the laity, that is, baptism" (*PL* 23, 158, c. 4). The Fathers and the Doctors of the Church, both those in the East and those in the West, have taught this truth explicitly. Irenaeus said that "all the just have the priestly order" (*Adv. Haer.*, 4, 8, 3). Chrysostom was even more direct and more concrete: "Thou wert made a priest at Baptism" is his unqualified presentation of the fact in his commentary on St. Paul's Epistle to the Corinthians (Hom. 3 — *PG* 61, 417). Augustine, as you might expect, places you "in Christ Jesus," for he was a realist to whom the Mystical Body of

Christ was the world's greatest Reality. In his *City of God* he wrote: "We say that all Christians are priests, seeing that they are members of the One Priest" (*PL* 41, 272).

Your possession of this magnificent gift from God — your priesthood — may puzzle you at first. So let St. Thomas Aquinas tell you that "the whole rite of the Christian Religion is derived from Christ's priesthood. Consequently, it is clear that the sacramental character is specially the character of Christ, to whose character the faithful are likened by reason of the sacramental characters, which are nothing other than *certain participations of Christ's Priesthood,* flowing from Christ Himself" (III, 63, 3).

The character that was stamped on your soul at Baptism was a priestly character. It was stamped there more indelibly, if such a thing were possible, by your Confirmation. More than likely you have always known that you had these "characters" in your soul. But just as likely you never knew exactly what they were, nor why they were. So listen to Matthias Joseph Scheeben, who has been called "the greatest genius among nineteenth-century theologians." "All characters," he says, when talking about those conferred by Baptism, Confirmation, and Holy Orders, "empower and oblige us to participate in greater or lesser degree in Christ's acts of worship. Above all, the character conferred by Holy Orders so conforms the priest to re-enact the Sacrifice of Christ. . . . But the Baptismal character enables all others, if not to re-enact, at any rate to offer the Sacrifice to God as their own, as a Sacrifice truly belonging to them on the strength of their membership in the Body of Christ. . . . Every character anoints and consecrates us to *active participation in the priesthood of Christ,* that divine priesthood to which His humanity was ordained by the hypostatic union" (*Mysteries of Christianity* [St. Louis: Herder, 1946], p. 586).

"Active participation in the priesthood of Christ . . ." that is the truth you must burn into your being; for that tells you, with scientific exactness, just what you are, and what you are to do at Mass. It enables you to understand just what Pius XI was exhorting you to in his *Miserentissimus Redemptor* when he wrote:

"In the very august Eucharistic Sacrifice, the priests and the rest of the faithful must join their immolation in such a way that they offer themselves as living hosts, holy and agreeable to God . . . they must concur in this oblation almost in the same manner as the priest." Scheeben's phrase will also enable you to understand what Pius XII meant when, in his *Mediator Dei,* he said: "Let the faithful learn to what a high dignity they have been raised in the Sacrament of Baptism"; as well as what St. Leo the Great had in mind when he exclaimed: "Recognize, O Christian, your dignity. . . . Keep in mind of what Head and what Body you are a member."

You may wonder why so little has been said to you about this marvelous prerogative of yours heretofore. The explanation is historical, and can be very enlightening. The fact is that some four hundred years ago a few men of influence took the phrase "the priesthood of the laity" and used it in such a way as to make it the rallying cry for those who would finally separate from the Church. Martin Luther once said: "All Christians are priests, and all priests are Christians.' Which is true enough as it stands, and can be explained in a perfectly orthodox sense. But Luther did not stop there. He went on to say: "Anathema to him who distinguishes the priest from the simple Christian." There you see the slyness and subtlety of Satan. Poor Martin Luther had been led on to exaggerate; and exaggeration always holds error. Never was the old saying about "he who proves too much, proves nothing" shown to be more true. For, in exaggerating the priesthood of the laity, Luther was actually denying all priesthood; for he was denying the priesthood of Holy Orders, the priesthood that consecrates. Hence, he was doing away with Mass. For to offer Mass is the prime function of priesthood. But since no Mass can be offered unless there is a consecration, to deny the priesthood that consecrates is to deny all priesthood. Take away Mass, and what is left of genuine Christian worship? The heart of the Church would be stilled. The Mystical Body would become very like the Corpse of Christ that first Good Friday night.

It was against this teaching that the Council of Trent pronounced some of its anathemas, one of which was leveled very explicitly against those who would dare to say that "all Christians share in the priesthood of Christ in the same manner." For the next four centuries theologians remained satisfied, for the most part, to repeat what was explicit in that anathema, without adverting to all that lies implicitly therein. To say that "all Christians do not share in the priesthood of Christ in the same manner" is to say that all Christians do share in the priesthood in different manners.

This was the truth that Pius XII taught with some fire during his last few years on earth. For, in his *Mystici Corporis,* an encyclical which marks very definitely the end of one epoch and indicates the beginning of another, he wrote: "In this Act of Sacrifice through the hands of the priest, whose words alone have brought the Immaculate Lamb to be present on the altar, the faithful, with one desire, and one prayer, offer it to the Eternal Father" (§ 97).

In that one sentence you have three truths which can clarify your duty at Mass, integrate your life, and awaken you to your possession of a transcendent dignity which you can never lose. For Pius XII teaches first, you are a priest — for only a priest can do what he says: offer Mass; second, you do this through the hands of the ordained priest, who alone has brought the Victim to the altar; third, your priesthood, while real, differs in function from that of the man who has received Holy Orders: he consecrates, you offer . . . with him and through him.

That would seem clear enough, but there were enthusiasts who exaggerated the Pontiff's true teaching. That is why you will read, in his *Mediator Dei,* passages which, at first blush, read like contradictions of the very explicit truth taught in the *Mystici Corporis.* But Pius XII did not contradict himself. He simply so clarified his former teaching that no one, hereafter, can exaggerate it with any possibility of winning credence.

Put in briefest form, the Pope insisted on what we have been pointing out in this chapter: the man in Orders consecrates; those, baptized and confirmed, can only offer. After stating emphatically that "the people . . . can in no way possess the sacerdotal power, that is, *the power to consecrate,*" the Pope proceeds to almost belabor the other truth, for, after citing previous pontiffs and some doctors of the Church regarding your priestly power, he turns to the Canon of the Mass itself and shows that you should never be merely passive during the Sacrifice if you want to be what you really are, and do what God appointed you to do. Then he concludes his argument by saying: ". . . it is indicated more than once (in the prayers of the Canon) that the people also participate in this august Sacrifice *inasmuch* as they offer the same. Nor is it to to be wondered at that the faithful should be raised to this dignity. By the waters of Baptism, as by common right, Christians are made members of the Mystical Body of Christ, the Priest, and by the 'character' which is imprinted on their souls, they are appointed to give worship to God. Thus they participate, according to their condition, in the priesthood of Christ" (§ 88).

How that truth should thrill! How it should change everyone's attitude toward Mass. For once you realize that you *are* a priest, you will know with finality that though you may be outside the sanctuary physically, you are never outside the action going on within the sanctuary really; that while you follow every action of the celebrating priest with sharp eyes, and listen to his every word with acute ears, you are anything but an onlooker or a mere listener. You are ever and always a participant in the actions, and say "Amen" to every word; for those words are, and that action is, *yours.* Pius X urged all "not to say prayers at Mass, but to pray the Mass." You can make this sainted Pontiff's directive even more direct as you resolve to do your "chief duty," and express your "supreme dignity" by always *"saying* Mass."

That does not mean that you must use the Missal and say every word that the priest at the altar says. It simply means that you are to develop a keen spiritual consciousness of who you are, and grow steadily in the realization of what you are to do at Mass: you *offer* the Christ of God to God — through the hands of the officiating priest, it is true, but you *truly* offer.

This fact may enable you to answer a question which already may have arisen in your own mind, and which you more than likely will hear from others: If you merely had to *hear* Mass, *be present* at Mass, or *attend* Mass, why would not a Mass heard and seen by you on television satisfy your obligation? You most certainly can see the priest and his actions much more clearly than you can in church. You most certainly can hear his words ever so much more clearly. Then why does not such sight and hearing, sharp and clear as it is, satisfy your obligation? Because you do not *participate* in that Mass which is on TV; you do not *offer* it; you cannot be *active* in it; for you are not a member of that priestly assemblage which is there with the officiating priest offering the Sacred Victim through his hands and in union with him. Of course you could offer this TV Mass spiritually; but you would not be able to offer it actually, for you would not be in a position to exercise fully the priesthood that is yours. To do that you have to be one of the "congregation" actually and physically present to and with the officiating priest.

Once we look upon a "congregation" and see it for what it is, there comes to us a grateful realization of the sacredness of every baptized person, the almost unbelievable wonder of the Mystical Body, and a consciousness of the closeness of God that is next to breathtaking. Take the pastor's description we have already used, look into the depth of reality, and watch how the picture changes.

He saw the children as fidgety. He saw correctly. But he only looked at the surface, at mere externals. Those fidgety children are priests of God; despite their fidgeting, they are actually offering God to God; despite their youth they are performing the greatest deed that can be performed by man. What is an orbital flight, a successful probe of Venus, Mars, Saturn, or the Moon, compared to what those fidgety children are doing? They go beyond all moons, stars, suns, on to the very throne of God; and they go there with Infinity in their hands. This they can do because they are priests.

Look at the young people whom the pastor described as "talking." These young people are wrong, of course; for they should be talking to God rather than to one another. Yet, their presence there in that priestly assembly says more to God than what they are saying to one another; and God, the All-Seeing, sees them far differently than does their pastor who looks on them merely as youngsters "talking." God sees them — and this is the truth of all truths not only for these youngsters, but for each of us — God sees them "in Christ Jesus" and, therefore, recognizes them as His only-begotten Son. He recognizes them as Christ in His Priestly action — and He loves them.

The same is true of the men who are "waiting for the end" — and the women who are "looking at their neighbors' dresses." All these people whom the pastor found "bored" are priests of God gathered to fulfill their priestly function. One can justly suppose that this "boredom" would never have come into being had the members of this particular assembly been made conscious of their priesthood; been made aware, as Pius XII expressly stated they should be made aware, that "to *participate* in the Eucharistic Sacrifice is their *chief duty and supreme dignity.*"

To participate. How we need to meditate on that word, to distill every last drop of meaning from it! Once we do that, we will "taste and see that the Lord is sweet"; for active participation as priests in the Sacrifice of Christ brings us into as intimate a contact, as complete a union, with God as is possible this side of eternity. What else is the hunger and thirst of our souls; what else is that fire burning in our being which we call desire; what is that dynamism, recognized or unrecognized, that creates in us a perpetual unrest, but our longing for God? Augustine finally analyzed it in his own case, and spares you and me the necessity for that soul-probing we find in his *Confessions.* Your heart and my heart, as well as the heart of Augustine — and the Immaculate Heart of Mary — were made for God "and will never know rest until they rest in Him." Thank God they can know some semblance of that ultimate "rest" when at Mass.

To participate. That means to take part. Part connotes a whole.

You are part of the one Mystical Body of Christ. It is the Mystical Body that you see when you look upon an assembly gathered for the celebration of Mass. The Mystical Body is the Body of Christ the Priest. Hence, its chief duty and supreme dignity is to offer the Holy Sacrifice.

To know just what it means to be a priest, and learn just how precisely you are one with Christ and united with God, take the definition of a priest and see how it applies first to Christ Himself, then to the priest who consecrates, and finally to the faithful. "A priest is one called and anointed by God to offer the Eucharistic Sacrifice." There are three elements in that definition: the call, the anointing, and the precise purpose of both, namely the offering of the Eucharistic Sacrifice. Each is absolutely necessary. Now apply that definition. . . .

Christ was called. In the Psalms and in the Epistle to the Hebrews you hear Him answering that call. "Here I am," He says, "I have come to do thy will, O God" (Ps 39:7; Heb 10:5). He was anointed priest at His conception by what theologians call "the grace of union." You know when, where, and how He exercised His priesthood: in the Cenacle there was the sacerdotal offering or *oblation* when, under the symbols of bread and wine, He offered His Body and Blood; on Calvary there was the mactation or *immolation,* when He underwent all He had promised in that oblation of the Cenacle — His Body was given, His blood poured out, He died the death; finally, there was the *acceptation* by God the Father, made manifest by the Resurrection, Ascension, and Enthronement of Christ at the Father's right hand.* There Christ is today as Eternal *Theotyte* — that is, as One given to, and accepted by, God as Sacrifice. There He is as the "Lamb slain from the beginning of the world" as "the First and the Last and the Living One," who says: "I was dead, but how wonderful, I live for ever and ever" (Ap 1:17, 18). It is because He is a living

---

* This is the theory of Maurice de la Taille, S.J. There are other theories about the relation of the Cenacle to Calvary, but this one appeals most to your author.

Theotyte that there can be Mass upon earth. Hence, there is need for men called by God, anointed by God, to offer this Eternal *Theotyte*. There is need for priests.

The priest at the altar who consecrates for you and thus brings down the living God, the ever loving *Theotyte,* under the appearances of bread and wine, was called by God. He had a vocation. He answered it. That it was genuine was recognized by the bishop who called him up to the altar to be anointed with chrism. With that anointing came the commission "to offer Sacrifice." There can be no question about his priesthood; every element of the definition is found in him.

What about you? You received a call from God to join His people. You answered it by receiving Baptism. That Sacrament was your "ordination," your "anointing," your receiving the power to offer the Eucharistic Sacrifice. As Christ carries about in His Body the five signs of His Priestly Sacrifice, so you carry in your soul your warrant to offer that same Sacrifice; for stamped thereon is the character of Christ's priesthood which neither time nor eternity can ever wear away. It tells that you have been called by God, anointed by God, and appointed by God to offer, through the ministry of the ordained priest, and in union with him, the "Pure Victim, the Holy Victim, the Immaculate Victim," called Jesus Christ, and "through Him, with him, and *in Him*" — yourself.

That makes you something of a temporal *theotyte* — a someone who has been offered to God as sacrifice, and accepted by Him as His own. Hence, you are not only one who is holy, but one who is literally sacred. But, *noblesse oblige* — how can you live up to your dignity? Mass is the answer — the only answer; for therein you exercise your priesthood, and prove that you are one "chosen from among men and appointed to serve men in what concerns the worship of God" (Heb 5:1).

Homo — res sacra: "Man — a sacred being." That is something seldom said about man today. Yet it is true with the truth of God, and especially true of you as a priest of God. Look at this analogy to see how *sacred* you are. . . .

The humanity, which the Second Person assumed, became the *conjoined instrument* by which, through which, and in which God effected the Redemption of mankind, by offering Mass. We adore that humanity; for it is the humanity of God. It is sacred with the sacredness of God.

Now the ordained priest bears some analogy to that humanity Christ assumed from the flesh and blood, bone and sinew of Mary Immaculate to be His "conjoined instrument" in the work of Redemption. For Christ "assumes," as it were, the humanity of this priest to be His "conjoined instrument" in the application of the fruits of Redemption, an application which is made chiefly through the Sacrifice of Mass. In Mass, you know, Christ is the principal offerer. He is the principal Priest who offers through the instrumentality of His ordained ministers. How close to the Son of God that makes the ordained man; analogously as close as was the Body and Blood He used to effect Redemption. How sacred is the priest!

How sacred are you! For you have been "assumed" from the mass of humanity into a vital union with Christ the Priest, to be His "conjoined instrument," to offer with Him, through the ministry of the ordained priest, the one Sacrifice of the New Law: His Mass and *yours*.

CHAPTER THREE

YOUR HANDS ARE FILLED — WITH GOD!

"He who comes to me will never hunger, and he who believes in me will never thirst" (Jn 6:36).

As the priest at the altar, who is actually presiding over an assembly of priests, says after the Offertory: *Orates fratres . . .* "Pray brethren that my Sacrifice and *yours* be acceptable . . ." do you realize that he is speaking the literal truth? This Sacrifice *is* yours.

The thoughtful, but not fully instructed, layman might well ask you how that can be when all you do is sit outside the sanctuary and watch that priest within the sanctuary performing all the actions in the celebration of what you call Mass. How is it your Sacrifice when all the words are spoken by another, all the gestures made by another, all the prayers pronounced by another? With what validity is this Action called yours, when you do not seem to act at all? You kneel, sit, and stand, it is true; but, all in all, there seems to be much more passivity to you than activity. You seem simply to watch and wait while this Action is being performed.

If that were all you actually did at Mass, there would be real reason for asking how the Sacrifice is yours; but there would be no reason for asking why you got so little out of Mass, or why you did not become more holy through Mass. For while it could justly be said that you had "heard Mass," had "been present at Mass," had "gone to Mass," it could never be said that you had *offered* Mass, or that you had *said* Mass. You would have observed the precept of the Church concerning one element in your observance of the Sabbath or holyday of obligation, but you would never have known that intimacy God meant you to know when He made you a priest and empowered you to offer Mass.

Consciousness of your dignity as priest and keen awareness of the personal power this prerogative gives you must be yours in a vivid, vital manner if Mass is to be that most intimate experience of meeting the God-Man all but face to face, of holding Him in your hands, and being able to lift Him up to the Father as perfect adoration, infinite gratitude, complete reparation, and as that Intercessor who cannot be refused. Unless you develop this consciousness you may go on wondering all your days just how the Holy Sacrifice is *yours*.

Viewing mere externals, this bit of wondering appears anything but groundless; for it is the priest at the altar who uncovers the chalice, puts the pall aside, lifts the paten which holds the host, and makes offering saying: *Suscipe Sancte Pater* — "Receive, all-holy Father, this spotless host which I, thy unworthy servant, offer Thee, my living and true God, for my countless sins. . . ."

That magnificent prayer seems exclusively the prayer of the priest at the altar. True it is that toward the end of it when he includes "all here present, as well as all the faithful Christians living and dead"; but the verb, the operative word in the sentence, is in the singular: "I [the priest at the altar] offer . . ."

It is a fact that this same priest will shift to the plural while mingling a few drops of water with the wine he is about to offer, and that he will say a prayer which tells tersely, truly, triumphantly, just what Mass is as it describes the "wondrous exchange." It runs: "O God, who in creating man didst wonderfully exalt his nature, and who has even more wonderfully refashioned it; by this Mystery, signified in the mingling of this water and wine, grant us a share in His Divinity, who has deigned to share our humanity." The plural is there throughout; the "exchange" is specified. But it is only the officiating priest who says this official prayer, and it will be only the officiating priest who will lift up that chalice which holds the water and the wine. Finally, it is only the officiating priest who will tell God that it is being offered to Him "for our salvation and that of the entire world." So the question remains: How is it your Sacrifice? Where is your part in it all? When, where, and how do you show yourself a priest?

Of course you may reply that Mass is an Act which is filled to the full with signs and symbols that really signify, and that you are symbolized in that water which has just been mingled with the wine and offered to God. That is absolutely correct. But where did you act in the offering? When did you perform any priestly function? Is this the only way you are made one with the officiating priest?

These questions are pointed and personal. For we all need to face such queries to quicken our consciousness that Mass is ours — each and every one of us in any group gathered in Church for the celebration of the Holy Sacrifice. For such a gathering is an assembly of God's "holy people," of God's "nation of priests"; and Mass is the sacred Action of God's community, Christ's Mystical Body, which is meant to live and act as a true community, as one Body, under the presidency and the headship of the officiating, ordained priest. So it will pay us all to examine this question; and examine it with vigor: How is Mass *yours?*

No one, of course, will question the fact that when the officiating priest lifts the paten with the wheat and the chalice with the wine and makes prayerful offering, that he is performing priestly action. But how is that action *yours?*

The celebrant alone offers the host, and the celebrant alone offers the wine. And he designates what he offers with precise words: *hanc immaculatam hostiam* — "this spotless host," and *calicem salutaris* — "this chalice of salvation." He says nothing about himself being in that host or in that chalice. He says nothing about you being in that water now mixed with the wine. And rightly so. For this host and this chalice with its water and wine will have the meaning of Mass only after the substance of wheat and the substance of wine has been yielded up and Jesus Christ, the God-Man, eternal Son of the eternal Father, with His glorious Body and Blood, His all-adorable human soul and His ever adorable Divinity has taken His place beneath the appearances of this Host and beneath the appearances of that Wine with its commingled water. For Mass is the offering to the Godhead of the Son of God made Man with all the infinite merits He won on Calvary. Let it never be forgotten that there is only one Victim in this Holy Sacrifice; for it was only the Spotless Lamb of God who shed His Blood for the remission of our sins. Hence, the officiating priest is most exact and correct in mentioning only the wheat and wine in his offering, and making no mention whatsoever of himself or of you. Bossuet put it with precision when he said: "We present Jesus Christ to God as our unique Victim and our unique Expiator by His Blood, protesting that we have nothing to offer to God but Jesus Christ and the infinite merit of His death."

What we must realize is that there is only one offering in Mass, as there is only One who is offered — Jesus Christ. But there are two places in the prayers of Mass which tell explicitly of this offering: one is at that which is known officially as the Offertory — when the officiating priest offers the bread and wine, as we have just seen; the other is after the Consecration — when the officiating priest offers the transubstantiated Bread and Wine. Hence, it is evident that the two offering prayers are about the One Offering — Jesus Christ. So let there be no confusion as we persist in the probing of the question: How is the Sacrifice *yours?* In what way do you act as *priest?* Your priesthood must center about the offering; for you are only an "offering priest." Where do you function as such?

The Fathers of the Council of Trent, guided by the Holy Spirit, taught emphatically that Mass is not a new Sacrifice made by Christ, but the selfsame Sacrifice He made on the Cross. More than likely you have memorized this truth and spoken it again and again, saying that Mass is the selfsame Sacrifice because it is offered by the same Priest (Christ), who offers the same Victim (Christ); the manner of offering alone being different. On Calvary it was in a bloody manner; in Mass it is in an unbloody manner.

You've heard it. You've memorized it. You've said it. You've

given unquestioning assent to it. But have you ever caught all that
is implied in this terse explanation by Trent? Have you ever heard
all the Conciliar Fathers left unsaid?

Christ lived in time on earth. Christ died in time and was buried
in the earth. Christ rose from the dead in time and showed Himself alive on earth for full forty days. Then, in time, Christ rose
from the earth, and was enthroned in eternity; enthroned as
Theotyte — that is, as Victim of Sacrifice accepted by God, and
thus made eternal Victor-Victim. But my Mass this morning was
in time, and on earth — away from both of which Christ, the
Offerer, the Offered, and the Offering, has gone. How did He get
back on earth and into time? — Only through the instrumentality
of my priesthood.

Had I not lent Jesus Christ my breath this morning, lent Him
my hands, my lips, my mind, my will, my whole being, so that He
might offer Himself through me, and speak the words of Consecration through my vocal organs, all-powerful God though He be,
He could not have come beneath the appearances of the host I
placed on my paten, nor beneath the appearances of the wine I
poured into my chalice. Almighty God needed me for the Mass
He offered through me this morning. Without me, of course, He
would have stood before God as Victor-Victim, and gone on making intercession for us in heaven; but, without me, He could never
have offered Mass from the altar before which I stood, nor at the
moment when I acted as His "conjoined instrument." You see,
then, what the ordained priest means to Jesus Christ. Actually,
Christ cannot live on earth sacramentally and sacrificially without
him. My hands were filled with God this morning. In a very real
sense it depends upon me whether they shall be filled with Him
again tomorrow morning.

But how does that help you answer the question which is, by
now, beginning to be something of a burning one: How is Mass
yours? In what way do you act as priest? — It gives the only
answer; for in my Mass this morning Christ was the Principal
Offerer; I, His "conjoined instrument" and secondary offerer. So

would you have been had you been there at my Mass; for you would have made the offering through me. I would have accepted a mandate, as it were, from you, by your very presence, to act in your name, to be your presiding officer, at this celebration, which would be a cooperative affair. The wheat offered would not have been of your growth nor of mine, neither would it have been of our gathering. The same of the wine; it would not have been of our vinting. Yet they would have been offered not as symbols of us in the first place, but to be offered, ultimately, as Christ offered the bread and wine in the Cenacle — as *His* Body and *His* Blood in Sacrifice. Yet they would have been our offerings, too. For we both would have had the intention of *doing* "in Christ Jesus" what He now does before the throne of God. As I was the extension of Christ inasmuch as He acted through me, so I would have been the extension of your hands, since I would have been holding up the host in your name; and both of us would be offering to God that which soon would be the God-Man, "in whom, through whom, and with whom" we, too, would be offered to God the Father in the unity of the Holy Spirit, to give Them "all honor and glory."

We are deep in the mystery of Christ now, and deep in the Mystery of Mass. We are also in the very depths of the sacredness which is ours "in Christ Jesus." He is the Priest *par excellence,* the Only Priest of the New Law. I am priest by His Sacrament of Holy Orders. You are priest by the ordination you received in Baptism. And all three of us offer to God "this most pleasing Sacrifice of praise." Christ, now, is never separated from His members. Consequently, we not only offered, but we were offered; for Mass is the offering of the Whole Christ: Head and members. It is the one priestly offering of the New Law — and it is offered by all of us, in our specific ways, who have been given some participation in the one priesthood of Jesus Christ.

Look closely at the similarities and the differences between the Cenacle, the Cross, and the Mass. In the Cenacle Christ did what we do at Mass: He took bread, blessed, broke, gave, saying: "This is My Body." We do the same in every Mass. But in the Cenacle

He added what we can never add: ". . . which shall be given for you." In Mass we offer that Body as already given — and accepted; that Body as it now is: glorious and immortal. On the Cross Christ gave Himself as He was then: in His physical Body. He offered Himself alone. In Mass the same Christ gives Himself as He now is: in His physical, glorified Body, which is the Head of His Mystical Body. Hence, when He offers Himself now, it is not as One alone, but as He now is — joined to all His mystical members. So in every Mass you and I are offered "in Christ Jesus."

Let us note, however, that this kind of "offering" is not your action nor mine. We are offered in every Mass the world over; but we do not function in every Mass as priests. Certainly I do not "consecrate" every host offered. Nor do I immediately "offer" every host that is to be consecrated — neither do you. It is only in those particular Masses in which you deliberately unite yourself with Christ and with His consecrating priest before you, that you function as "offering priest." That is why Pope Pius XII warned you in his great encyclical on the Liturgy: "The faithful must not be content to take part in the Eucharistic Sacrifice by the general intention which all the members of Christ and the children of the Church ought to have; they ought also, in the spirit of the Liturgy, unite themselves closely and of set purpose with the High Priest (Christ) and His minister on earth (the priest who consecrates)" (*Mediator Dei,* § 104).

How do you do that? Not by words only, but by acts of your will, acts of your heart, your soul, your whole being. By putting meaning into the Offertory by offering yourself, all you have, all you are to God "in Christ Jesus." You can do that in no better way than by using the very words I use at the altar, and using them at the same time. It is not absolutely essential that you do so; but it is essential, if you are going to offer Mass as a priest, that you act "in Christ Jesus," through Him, and with Him.

What does all this sublimate to? — Acts of your intellect and will; the highest acts of which you, as a human are capable. But this offering as priest will be no mere human act; it will be elevated by grace to a realm far beyond the human. You will be acting as a son of God in God's only Son, through His all-holy Spirit. You will act as every priest acts when performing his sacerdotal function: you will act in the Trinity. You will be in the universe of the Divine. For Mass, in ultimate analysis, is an Act of God. Strictly speaking, no man can offer Mass. Only the God-Man can. But He does so through chosen men who freely yield themselves to be His instruments. You are one such. . . .

Therefore, you should be awake at the Offertory: wide awake! and awake to yourself as a priest of God. So that by specific acts of will and intellect you can place yourself on the paten with the wheaten bread and in the chalice with the water mingled with the wine, realizing all the while whom this wheat and wine represent now and to whom they will soon yield their substance. Then you can offer Christ Jesus to God the Father and "in Christ Jesus" yourself. That will be exercising your priesthood "according to your condition," and really making this Sacrifice *your own*.

The wheat and wine have little or no intrinsic value, but, even at the Offertory, they are laden heavily with meaning. They mean Christ. They mean you. They mean me. They mean the whole Mystical Body, the entire Church, from reigning Pontiff to latest baptized infant. They will receive value at the Consecration — and it is for consecration that we really offer them. It is for "consecration" that we really offer ourselves! Hence, the weightless wafer of wheat and the almost measureless amount of wine have personal meaning and are heavy with purpose even for us at the Offertory. How much more so after Consecration! Then we really offer ourselves "in Christ Jesus."

Again I beg you not to be confused by the fact that I speak of offering bread and wine at the Offertory proper, then tell you to offer the living Jesus Christ present under the appearances of bread and wine after the Consecration. These are not two different offerings. Mass is but a *single* Offering — Jesus Christ. But He is in our hands really only after the Consecration. He was in our hands at the Offertory proper only symbolically. Hence, after the

Consecration we will offer Him as He actually is: living, loving, glorious Head of the Mystical Body; consequently, "in Him, with Him, and through Him" we will offer ourselves and all His members. Hence you will want to say with the priest who has consecrated:

> Wherefore, O Lord, we Thy servants, and with us Thy holy people, calling to mind the blessed passion of this same Christ Thy Son, Our Lord, likewise His resurrection from the grave and glorious ascension into Heaven, offer to Thy Sovereign Majesty, out of the gifts Thou hast bestowed upon us, a pure Victim, a holy Victim, a spotless Victim, the sacred Bread of everlasting life, and the Chalice of eternal salvation. . . .
>
> Humbly we ask Thee, God Almighty, to command that these be carried by the hands of Thy Holy Angel up to Thy altar on high, to the sight of Thy divine majesty, so that those of us who, by partaking of the Sacrifice of this altar, shall have received the sacred Body and Blood of Thy Son, may be filled with every heavenly blessing and grace; through the same Christ our Lord. . . .
>
> Through whom, O Lord, Thou dost always create, sanctify, endow with life, bless and bestow upon us all these, Thy gifts. Through Him, and with Him, and in Him, be unto Thee, O God the Father Almighty, in the unity of the Holy Spirit, all honor and glory, world without end.

Therein you have the perfect and precise expression not only of who you are and what you are, but also of what you are doing and why you are doing it. Thanks to such prayers you can offer Mass properly by making full and intelligent use of your share in the priesthood of Jesus Christ.

Those prayers also clarify what may, at first, have confused you; for they tell you in unmistakable language that the gifts given you by God, the wheat and wine lifted up to God at the Offertory, were lifted up for only one purpose: to be the One Gift which is Mass — Jesus Christ, His only Son, and in Him all His mystical members.

If you have reason to be wide awake at the official Offertory, you have twice the reason to be even more wide awake at the offertory made after the Consecration; for here is He, who is Mass, in His total Act of Love. Generous Lover that He is, He places

Himself in your hands just as He now is — in full and complete surrender of love. — He gives you Himself: glorified, all-adorable, perfect Man, all-true God. He gives you Himself to be offered to the Father. He surrenders Himself into your hands so that you can act as priest, make His Sacrifice yours. Truly, at Mass, your hands are filled with God.

As you see, the exercise of your priesthood rests on faith. The more lively your faith, the more vivid your consciousness of your priesthood, the higher will flame your fire of love for Jesus Christ and His Mass. Since that flame will rise and fall in accord with the varying degrees of your consciousness of your priesthood, I say to you what Paul once said to his beloved Timothy: "Stir up God's grace of office which you have" (2 Tim 1:16). In other words, stir up your faith.

It is here that faith is tested as nowhere else. Wheat and wine weigh every human being in the balance which means eternal life. Mass is the *Mysterium Fidei* — the "stumbling block" over which the Jews fell, the "absurdity" at which the Gentiles scoffed, but "to us who have been called, Christ the power of God and the wisdom of God" (1 Cor 1:23, 24). To us who have been made priests, Mass is the coming of Christ in Person, the living, glorified Jesus, who comes to be THE Gift we can offer to God. He comes to love us, to love us to life — His own Life — by making that "wondrous exchange." But even then we have not said all. Christ comes to be our Food and Drink.

You will never come to a vital realization of what Mass is until you hear those words about Food and Drink ring with all the resonances they held the day Christ first spoke them at Capharnaum. Jesus Christ, whom we so often designate as "the gentle Jesus," opened His discourse to the Jews with words that were anything but gentle. Reading the sixth chapter of St. John, we learn that yesterday Jesus had multiplied five barley loaves and two fishes to feed five thousand men. That night He had walked on the waters of Lake Tiberias, joined the disciples who were battling rising seas some three or four miles from shore, and, with them, crossed to Capharnaum. In the morning the Jews who had fed on the multiplied loaves and fishes crossed the sea to look for Jesus. When they found Him and let Him know they had been looking for Him, He very bluntly said: "I tell you the plain truth: you are looking for me, not because you saw manifestations of power, but because you partook of the loaves and made a hearty meal of them." That is not exactly an ingratiating exordium. Yet Jesus was about to teach them the truth of all truths, as is evident from His next sentence: "Do not be concerned about the food that is bound to perish, but about the food that affords eternal life — the food which the Son of Man will give you; for on him God the Father has set his seal of approval" (Jn 6:26, 27).

The Jews showed themselves pious Jews. They reacted to the mention of God the Father, and asked, with all sincerity, as we suppose, what it was that God required of them. "This is what God requires," said Jesus, "believe in his ambassador." They showed themselves willing to do this provided that Jesus would give them some sign as proof that He was God's ambassador, and reminded Him that Moses had given their fathers manna in the desert.

Then came the reply that shocked, but which was going to lead on to greater shock. "I tell you the plain truth," replied Jesus, "Moses did not give you the bread from heaven; not at all: my Father gives you the real bread from heaven; for only the bread that comes down from heaven for the purpose of giving life to the world is God's bread." To that the Jews made the only sensible reply possible: "Then let us always have the bread you speak of." But little did they expect the answer they were given. "I am the bread of life," replied Jesus, "he who comes to me will never hunger, and he who believes in me will never thirst. The pity is, as I said, you have seen me, and yet refuse to believe" (Jn 28–36).

Note that Jesus was asking for faith. He actually told them their faith was being tested, and they were failing in the test. But now let us read the ensuing lines in the light of all we have meditated on, our call, our dignity, our duty as priests, and see the destiny

that is ours if we go on answering that call, living that faith, being
that priest. Jesus went on: "Only one whom the Father entrusts
to me will come to me; and when anyone comes to me, I will not
reject him; for I have come down from heaven not to do my will,
but the will of him whose ambassador I am. Now this is the will
of him whose ambassador I am: I am not to lose anything of what
the Father has entrusted to me, but raise everything from the dead
on the last day. Yes, it is my Father's will that everyone who looks
at the Son and believes in him shall have eternal life and be raised
by me on the last day" (Jn 6.38–40).

You would expect such words to kindle in the Jews a veritable
will to believe. But no. They went on "grumbling at him for saying:
'I am the bread of life that has come down from heaven.' " They
knew His father and mother. To them this Jesus was the son of
Joseph, and Mary was his mother. How could he now say that
He "had come down from heaven." It was incredible.

It was not the Mystery of the Holy Eucharist that they were
denying; for that had not been revealed as yet. They were refusing
to believe that Jesus was God's ambassador; refusing to accept
Him as the Bread of faith — Eternal Truth. They kept grumbling:
"How can he say: 'I have come down from heaven'?"

Jesus answered them saying: "Do not grumble among yourselves. . . . I tell you the plain truth: he who believes is in possession
of eternal life. I am the bread of life. Your fathers ate the manna
in the desert, and they died. The bread which I speak of, which
comes down from heaven, is such that no man who eats of it will
ever die. I am the living bread that has come down from heaven.
If one eats of this bread, he will live forever; and furthermore,
the bread which I shall give you is my flesh given for the life of
the world" (Jn 6:43–51).

Twenty centuries of time have not softened the shock of these
words. Small wonder that John reports that "the Jews then had a
violent discussion among themselves. 'How,' they argued, 'can this
man give us his flesh to eat'?"

Jesus knew what was going on. Does He soften the blow? Far

from it. He delivers a heavier one. "Resuming, therefore, Jesus said to them: 'What I tell you is the plain truth: unless you eat the flesh of the Son of Man and drink his blood, you have no life in you. He who eats my flesh and drinks my blood is in possession of eternal life; for my flesh is real food, and my blood is real drink. He who eats my flesh and drinks my blood is united with me, and I am united with him. As the living Father has appointed me his ambassador, and I live because of the Father, so, too, he who eats me will have life because of me" (Jn 6:53–58).

What words to fall from the lips of a living man! No wonder "the result was that many of his disciples among his hearers said: 'Such language is hard to bear; who can listen to it!' But Jesus, inwardly aware that his disciples were grumbling on this account, said to them: 'Does this make you waver in your faith? Suppose, then, you see the Son of Man ascend to where he was before? The Spirit is the life-giving thing; the flesh as such is worthless. The words I have spoken to you are spirit and, therefore, life. The trouble is, there are some among you that have no faith" (Jn 6:60–64).

It had been the Jews who had first "murmured." Now some among his disciples "were grumbling," and "thereupon went back to their old life and would no longer associate with him." The Twelve are still left. Jesus turns to them, not with a plea, but with a challenge: "Are you, too, minded to go away?" It is a challenge of faith, a demand for a decision. Peter meets that challenge and makes that decision: "Master, to whom shall we go? You have a message of eternal life; we firmly believe and are fully convinced that you are the Holy One of God."

The Twelve did not understand the words of Jesus any more than the Jews or the disciples. Peter was just as dumbfounded and bewildered by these sayings of Jesus as were all the others. But he trusted the Master. He believed Him to be "the Holy One of God," and on the strength of that belief, accepted statements he could not understand. Faith had been rigorously tested — and it triumphed.

In Mass, Carpharnaum's test is given to you and to me. The Jesus, who stood before the crowd He had fed only yesterday by a miracle, stands before us in Mass and hurls the same unheard-of challenge at our minds, our hearts, our wills. He offers Himself to be our Food, our Drink, our Life. He uses no metaphor. True, at Capharnaum He did say: "The spirit is the life-giving thing; the flesh as such is worthless." But He did not mean that we are to feed on His spirit, slake our thirst with His spirit. His insistence at Capharnaum was on real flesh, real blood, real food, real drink. His reference to the spirit can only have been a reference to His Holy Spirit who, indeed, is "life-giving." But every word about His Flesh and His Blood is to be taken literally. It takes faith — lively, strong, sturdy faith. Capharnaum and Mass are faith's supremest testings. But as Christ told us more than once in this revelation at Capharnaum: Faith is a gift from the Father. But we well know that a gift becomes such only when it is accepted. You have to accept God's offer of faith freely, willingly, lovingly, gratefully. Then, as Christ Himself said: "you will have eternal life."

"How can this man give us his flesh to eat?" He could not were He only man. But this man is the God-Man. This Man whom you hold in your hands at Mass is Love — and Love does such things. Only Divine Love could do such things; for He alone can give not only what He has, but what He is.

Someone has remarked: "No earthly love is ever perfectly fulfilled. To love, in the earthly sense, really means to strive for the impossible." The Disciple whom we have been following, gives us clue to this reality when he shows us the total otherness of Christ's love; for he tells us in his First Epistle that Christ not only loves, but that He is love (1 Jn 4:8). That being the case, you can see that He is the only One who can truly love "His own who are in the world" and love them "to the end" — that is, completely, with the totality of His being, and the unconditional surrender that alone is real love. That is the God you truly hold in your hands at Mass, whom you offer with a sacerdotal offering; the God whom you actually encounter.

CHAPTER FOUR

THIS IS REALITY

"You shall see God . . . under the appearances of . . ."

"Encounter God." — Those words evoke fright in some, enthusiasm in others, skepticism in still others. Reaction they are sure to call forth; for, whether we realize it or not, to encounter God is the deepest and most insatiable yearning of our being. We were made to encounter God. Face it we must: that is going to be the ultimate reality of our lives — we are going to encounter Him one day as our Judge. If we have been wise enough and grateful enough to have made Mass our lives and our lives Mass, we will encounter Him face to face for all eternity as Lover. That will be heaven. That will be eternal bliss. But the claim made in these pages is that we encounter God in the present time — as Lover — in every Mass. The further claim is now made that this encounter is the reality of all realities this side of the grave.

I have said that you meet God in Mass; that you meet Him personally, and meet Him as a Person. Some may want to object and say: "Father, you are using words figuratively, are you not?" And my answer is: "Indeed I am not!" I mean exactly what I have said, and I mean it exactly: you meet God in Mass. You see God. You hear God. You touch and taste God. I long for you to realize this with as vivid a realization as our generous God will grant you; and I can assure you that if you show your love by a holy avidity for this realization, God will grant it to you in that measure of His which is actually measureless. I long for this for you, because my basic conviction is that you and others do not get all that you should out of Mass, nor become more and more holy through Mass simply because you do not live in the real universe of Mass. You are not in vital contact with real reality.

Eyebrows may go up, frowns may appear, as I insist that you meet God in Mass; that you see Him, hear Him, touch and taste Him. Maybe I can lower those brows, smooth away those frowns, by saying that I am not speaking figuratively at all, but that I am speaking, if you will allow the word and catch all that is meant by it, "sacramentally."

The college senior who led us into reality in the first chapter by his reply about bed when I questioned him as to his thoughts as he set out for Mass, is the same individual who will now lead us into deeper reality. For, when I told him he was going to *see* God in Mass, he frowned. But when I went on and asked him: "Where will you see Him first?" he brightened; for he had a ready reply. "In the Host," he said.

I had to tell him he was wrong. Of course he was absolutely right concerning his own subjective mentality. He would see God first in the Host. But according to objective reality he was very wrong; for he — and you — and I — and all of us should see God first in ourselves, then in the congregation assembled for Mass, then in the priest who will officiate, and only finally, in the Host.

If you can see God in the consecrated Host — and you most certainly can, if you have any faith at all; then you can see Him just as really in the baptized priests in the congregation, and in the ordained celebrant at the altar. For Jesus Christ is as really present in these as He is in that Host. In the Host, of course, He is sacramentally — and sacrificially — present. In the baptized and ordained he is present sacrificially — and mystically. The mode of being present is different; but that difference in mode does not alter the reality of the Presence.

When you speak of the "Real Presence" you believe, with all the force of your Catholic Faith, that you are speaking about Reality. You do not hesitate to say that "under the appearances of

Bread and Wine" you see Jesus Christ. That same Catholic Faith teaches, and you should assimilate the teaching, that there is another "real Presence" — in the members of the Mystical Body.

"Appearances are deceptive." No one will question the truth in that well-known axiom. But never did it hold such personal truth, such vital truth, such holy truth as when we apply it sacramentally and mystically. In Mass the wheat and wine look the same after Consecration as they did before. But were appearances ever so deceptive? Before I pronounce those "thunder-powered words" which the Son of God commanded me to pronounce in His name and in His Person, the wheat is almost weightless and the wine next to valueless — an ounce or so from a very inexpensive bottle. But after those words — what weight in that Wheat! What infinite value in that Wine. God is there. Or, more exactly, the God-Man is there.

Such exactness may be necessary for those literalists who will tell me that "no man can see God." Of course they are right if they mean God as He is, God in His essence; for God is the Purest of all pure spirits, the Simplest of all simple beings, and cannot be seen by bodily eyes. But God's Presence can be seen!

You have never laid eyes on your soul. You never shall. But will you tell me that you have never seen the *presence* of your soul? Look in your mirror and note the light in your eyes, the color in your face, the movement in your lips as you smile at the folly and fallacy of those literalists who say you cannot see God because He is a spirit. But if they persist in being literal, allow them the liberty, but beg them to allow you the light of your faith-filled eyes — and the ability to see with them "under the appearances . . ." your God.

The technical phrase is repeated, for it will lead us into reality perhaps better than anything else ever will — regarding Mass and this vision of God.

"You shall see God!" is what the Curé of Ars, St. John Vianney, used to say in one of his most effective sermons. Pointing his bony finger at his congregation, he would repeat that sentence again and again until he had his attentive hearers in something close to awe. He was referring to the Last Judgment. But I say the same thing to you as you set out for Mass: You shall see God! — but it will be in anything but the guise of judge.

You shall see God "under the appearances of" human flesh as you look at your fellow Christians gathered to offer God to God. He is there. Not "substantially," as He will be in the Host after Consecration; but there just as really. Open your eyes to reality, and in those fidgety children the pastor seemed to be complaining about, you will see Him who said: "Let the little children alone, and do not stop them from coming to me. The Kingdom of Heaven belongs to such as these" (Mt 19:14). In those young people the pastor saw talking, you will see Him whom ten lepers saw "as he entered a town" (Lk 17:19) and who called to Him to be made clean — and He made them clean; you will see Him whom Jairus begged to come to the bedside of his daughter who had just died — whom Christ returned to life saying: *Talitha cumi* — "Little girl, I command you awake" (Mk 5:41); you will see Him before whom Thomas bowed in the Cenacle one week after the Resurrection and called "My Master and my God" (Jn 20:29). In the fashionably dressed ladies who, according to the pastor, were eyeing their neighbors, you will see Him whom the Magdalen saw at Simon's banquet — and whose feet she washed with her tears; you will see Him whom the woman caught in adultery saw when she looked up after He had written in the dust — and from whom she received forgiveness; you will see Him whom the Samaritan woman saw weary and thirsty at Jacob's Well — and from whom she received the revelation that He was the Messias. In the men who are just waiting for the end, as the pastor said, you will see Him who loved His own who were in the world — and loved them to the end.

You will see Christ, the same Christ these people looked upon of old; but you will see Him as none of them saw Him before He had said His First Mass. Though St. Paul tells us that "Jesus Christ is the same, yesterday, today, and forever" (Heb 13:8), you will not see Him today as Nathaniel saw Him when he called Him

"Rabbi," nor as the young man saw Him who called Him "Good." You will see Him only as the Magdalen saw Him when she called Him "Rabonni." For it is the Risen Christ who is Head of the Mystical Body, who lives in His members, and in whom His members "live and move and have their being" (Acts 17:28). It is the Risen Christ who is present "under the appearances of" their flesh and blood, and it is "through Him, with Him, and in Him," the Risen Jesus, that these Christians will give God "all honor and glory," as they offer Mass. Hence, I urge you to open wide your eyes of faith and see the reality of all realities: "Christ loving Himself."

The leading killer of joy in the soul today is that lack of realism which produces spiritual myopia, and keeps us from seeing Christ where Christ really is — in each of the baptized about us. Bossuet may free us from this debility. Because he saw with utter clarity he could say with utter conviction: "The Church is Jesus Christ prolonged in space and time and communicated to men." John Gruden, one of our own American theologians, was equally clear-eyed. Hence he could say: "to separate Christ from the Church, or the Church from the Person of Christ, is to destroy the very essence of Christianity." These men looked at the Church, which is the living faithful, and saw the living Jesus Christ. "Under the appearances of" baptized Catholics they recognized Christ as our Contemporary.

Perhaps the dust raised by so-called intellectuals has got into the eyes of too many modern Catholics. These clever men have written so much about the "historical Christ," that some of them have come to look upon the Son of God as just another historical figure. Great, of course; perhaps the greatest in all history, they admit. But such an admission, while it is true, is far from the truth of Christ and Christianity. The point these would-be intellectuals miss is the central point of the Faith, and the point you must never miss; namely, that "the historical Christ" is a Man of our times. For the physical Christ who was seen long ago in Bethlehem, Nazareth, Jerusalem, and Capharnaum, and the Mystical Christ who is seen today in the Catholics of Boston, Beirut, Bombay, and Berlin, are not two distinct persons. That could never be; for, as we have already heard Paul saying: "Jesus Christ is the same yesterday, today, and forever" (Heb 13:8).

Look at yourself and your fellow Catholics gathered for Mass and see them for what they are: a miniature Mystical Body whose Head is the Incarnate Second Person of the Blessed Trinity, and whose Soul is the Holy Trinity's Third Person. Realize that just as God used the flesh and blood of Mary Immaculate to become incarnate in His physical Body, so He is using your flesh and blood and that of your fellow Catholics to prolong that Incarnation in His Mystical Body. Realize with the keenest realization possible that just as He needed that physical Body taken from Mary in order to offer His first and only Mass, so does He need you and your fellow Catholics who form His Mystical Body, in order to make that one and only Mass of His present to you at this time and in this place.

How near is God! How dear you and your fellow Catholics are to Him. How near and dear each member of the congregation assembled for Mass should be to you. Since they are Christ's members, they are Christ. See Him in them, and them in Him. Then you will be looking on true reality.

Of course you may tell me there are some in this congregation who are living anything but Christlike lives, and whose actions are anything but priestly. You may even be able to say with some certainty that some one or other is actually living in what is called the "state of sin." That does not alter the reality. If they have not been excommunicated, nor lost their Faith, they are still Christ's members. Dead members, it is true; but members who can be brought to life again. Dostoevski, the great Russian novelist, gives a doctrinally sound directive concerning such members when he says: "never look upon a sinner except with love; for thus, and thus only, can we most certainly be like God."

God looks upon every sinner with love. Perhaps never with greater love than when He sees such at Mass. For did not Christ

Himself state clearly: "It is my mission to call sinners, not saints" (Mk 2:17). And did He not say to the chief priests and the leaders of the people on Monday of the first Holy Week: "I tell you frankly, the tax-collectors and prostitutes are ahead of you in entering the kingdom of God" (Mt 21:31). How could anyone question Christ's love for sinners when about to offer that "memorial of His Passion" we call Mass when he recalls that Christ died for sinners — and that it is true that "greater love than this no man has" (Jn 15:13).

Christ rose that we should no longer sin, it is true, but if you should know some Catholics who, unhappily, are still in their sin, approach them reverently; for, so long as they are on earth, there is always a possibility for Christ to know within them something of a resurrection. Perhaps you, by being realist enough to offer this Mass this very morning as you should offer it, may make it Easter for Him in them, and for them in Him. Make St. Augustine's very wise observation your own: "there is no reason to despair of the health of whatever is still part of the body"; and sinners who have not been excommunicated, withdrawn from Holy Mother Church, or lost their faith, are still members of His Body.

"I saw God in a man," said a French peasant on his return from Ars after seeing John Vianney, the village Curé. Knowing now how holy that bony little priest was, we may be tempted to pass off this remark as a mere stressing of the obvious. But wait a moment. Not all who lived in Ars in those days, nor all who went to Ars, would have made the same remark. Many in the village looked upon the Curé as a meddlesome, somewhat cranky old priest. Many of those who visited Ars saw nothing more than an exceptionally pious and very zealous curé. But the peasant who said he "saw God in a man" saw reality. He saw what you and I should see every time we look upon a man who has recived Holy Orders, and most especially when we look upon him when vested for the Holy Sacrifice.

Do not argue that it would be easy to see God in a man such as the Curé of Ars, but that it would take something better than

20/20 spiritual vision to see God in some of the priests you know. For that is not being realistic. Remember we are now seeing *"under appearances"*; we are looking into the depths, and seeing Him who is there. We are face to face with God in Mass. Let us awake to reality and see Him where He is: in the people, in the priest, and — thanks to them — finally, in the Host.

I say "thanks to them" for Christ could not be in His Mystical Body had not your priest and your fellow Catholics given that assent of love we call faith. They had to assent as freely as did Mary before she was overshadowed by the Holy Spirit and the physical Body of Jesus began to take form within her. And never be unmindful of the fact that it is thanks to the same Holy Spirit that the Mystical Body of the same Jesus Christ is formed through you and your fellow Catholics. Finally, that "thanks to them" is most realistic when we turn to Mass; for it is only because your priest freely offered his hands to be chrismed that Jesus Christ can come in sacramental form and be present in the Host.

Surely you must have thought of John the Baptist some time or other as you watched your celebrating priest lift the Host and heard him say: "Behold the Lamb of God — Behold Him who takes away the sins of the world." It was the Baptist who first spoke those words as he one day saw Jesus coming toward him. More than likely you have come to look upon the Precursor as the greatest born of woman. It is almost inevitable — but it is a mistake. It is almost inevitable, I say, for Christ Himself praised John as no man has ever been praised by God. Jesus actually said: "I positively assure you: among all men born of women, no one has risen to greater heights than John the Baptist" (Mt 11:11).

Who would not concur after hearing of John's wondrous conception and learning about all the marvels that preceded and accompanied his birth. Who would look upon the Baptist in any other light after watching him spend his youth and early manhood in the desert, then seeing him come forth to electrify all Israel with his preaching? He so fired the people that the Sanhedrin was moved, and sent messengers to ask if he were the Christ. You know John's reply: "I am not the Christ."

That is a reply no ordained priest could give. Were you to ask the celebrant of any Mass: "Are you the Christ?" what could he say? — He has just bent over unleavened bread and said: "This is *My* Body" — and the Body of Christ was immediately there in his hands. Likewise he has just bent over a chalice of wine and said: "This is *My* Blood" — and immediately in that chalice was the Blood of Jesus Christ.

Am I insinuating that the ordained priest is greater than John the Baptist? No, indeed! I am not insinuating. I am stating it bluntly, boldly. Not only that, but I am adding that not only the priest who has been ordained by the Sacrament of Holy Orders, but you and every other person, male or female, who has been "ordained" by the Sacrament of Baptism is greater than John the Baptist. That is the effect that was brought about in the ontological order when the sacramental character was stamped on your soul and mine — that character which is the character of Christ the Priest. How dare I say such a thing? How dare I seemingly contradict Jesus Christ who said that "among all men born of women, no one has risen to greater heights than John the Baptist"? That is the point, the piercing point: I am not contradicting Jesus Christ who made the above statement; I am only echoing Him who followed that statement with the words: "In the kingdom of heaven, it is true, the least is greater than he [John the Baptist]" (Mt 11:11).

You may tell me that you have never been conscious of this greatness; and, no doubt, you would be telling me the truth. But psychological consciousness is one thing, ontological reality quite another. No newly born babe is psychologically aware that he or she has an immortal soul; but that lack of awareness does not change the ontological fact: he or she *has* an immortal soul. It is precisely this psychological awareness of ontological reality that we are striving to produce in you as we endeavor to show you one way of getting more out of Mass, and one way of becoming more holy through Mass. For the conviction deepens that it is precisely

this lack of psychological consciousness of their personal preroga-
tives, of their transcendent dignity, of the sacred power that is
theirs, that has produced apathetic and anemic Catholics.

Why do you think St. Paul was so persistent in writing about
being "in Christ Jesus"? Why did he tell his Romans that since
they "had died with Christ, they should also believe that they are
alive with Him" (6:8); why did he so unqualifiedly say to his
Corinthians that "if any man is in Christ, he is a new creation"
(2 Cor 5:17); why did he tell his Galatians that "what really
counts is being a new creature" (6:15); why did he command his
Colossians to "strip off the old self with its deeds and put on the
new . . . for Christ is everything in us" (3:10); why did he urge
his Ephesians to "renew themselves constantly by spiritual con-
siderations, and put on the new self, created after the image of
God in the justice and holiness that come from truth" (4:24)?
Does not all this add up to that one all-important command given
to the Romans, but meant for you, and me, and everyone born
of woman: *Induimini Dominum Jesum Christum* — "Put on the
Lord Jesus Christ" (Rom 13:14). But in the ontological order,
the order of being, of reality, we cannot "put on the Lord Jesus
Christ"; for He is already put on at Baptism. So what Paul was
exhorting us to is an ever keener psychological consciousness of
the ontological reality by frequent reflection, true recollection; by
thinking and willing; in short, by truly realizing that *we are Christ*.

What Paul wanted all of us to have, and what every single
Christian needs, is an awareness of the "wondrous exchange"
already effected by the Sacraments, and both promised and prayed
for by Christ Himself just before He offered His First Mass: that
we "come to *understand* that he is in the Father, and we are in
him, and he is in us" (Jn 14:20). Make Mass the Act of Love it
actually is and that further promise made by the same Christ at
the same time will also be fulfilled: "He that loves me will, in turn,
be loved by the Father; and I will love him, and manifest myself
to him" (Jn 14:21).

Look at reality and see its actuality in the psychological realm.

Some time ago I heard of a man who took an old frame from his attic and used it to hold a highly polished mirror he had just procured. It fitted perfectly, and even matched the woodwork near which he planned to hang it. The man was quite elated with his bit of "do-it-yourself." But when hanging the mirror he looked down at the base of the frame and found that someone had cut into it the single name: *CHRIST*. Undoubtedly the frame had held some picture of the God-Man before it was put in the attic. For a moment the man was hesitant. Was it proper, he wondered, to leave that holy name there while using the frame for this mirror. But then it came to him that when he looked into that mirror he should be seeing "under the appearances of" his own features none other than Him whose name had been carved into the frame. That is reality. That is theology. That is truth. Every time he looked into that mirror the name there recalled this man to reality, and gave him psychological awareness of actuality.

Whenever we use a looking glass why shouldn't we recall that every human being is an indestructible mirror who holds in his deepest heart the reflection of God the Creator, and that every validly baptized person is an irrefragable mirror that shows forth from its deepest depths the priestly countenance of Jesus Christ? Neither of those mirrors is untarnishable — humans can sin — but each is indestructible. For no human can ever cease to be an image of God. Psychological awareness can be increased, then, if every time you look in a mirror, you reflect on actual reality, and look deep enough to see "under the appearances of" your own human features Him who is *really* there — Jesus Christ. No one need be cautioned about being like the man St. James described "who looks into a mirror at the face nature gave him. He looks at himself, yes, but then he goes away, and at once forgets what he looks like" (1:24). See more than the face nature gave you; and never forget that you look like Jesus Christ!

Today in philosophy and theology, as well as in art and literature, "personalism" is in vogue. Basically it is a demand for sincerity. When kept within bounds this drive is good. So I dare say:

Be modern enough, when at Mass, to be sincerely personalistic. At Mass you should express yourself as completely as possible. That you will never do unless you realize who you are, and understand what you are to do. Actually, your soul surge is pointed to nothing so directly as to this. You want gestures that are truthful; speech that is genuine, simple, true; signs that signify and are clearly intelligible. In brief, you want an encounter with God. You have it ontologically; for that is what Mass is. But, perhaps, until now you have not had it psychologically, because you have never analyzed this phrase which is becoming so common that at times it sounds too glib: "to encounter God."

To encounter means "to meet." But to meet a person calls for a union of the distinct, even of the opposed. When you and I meet there is a union, a communion between two persons who are, and ever will remain, distinct. That union can take place in what is called the intentional order; that is, on the level of knowledge and love. I cannot love you until I know you. I cannot know you until I meet you, see you, hear you, and perhaps touch you. And I will never know you really unless I love you. Hence, two persons are said to meet one another only when there is mutual knowledge and love.

You do not meet all those who happen to be physically present to you. You do not meet each of those who ride the subway with you on your way to work; nor each of those who happen to attend the same lecture, concert, show, or spectacle you go to. Physical proximity may allow for some semblance of oneness, but there is no real, personal union or communion unless there is mutual exchange, mutual knowledge, mutual love.

Therefore, if there is to be anything at all to all this talk about "encountering God" and "meeting Christ" in Mass, there must be some direct knowledge of the actual fact, and consequent love. I must know that Christ and I are meeting; for the meeting of persons is a psychological event. Hence, there must be consciousness of contact, or there is no real meeting. That is why I made bold to use St. John's words: "We proclaim . . . what we have heard, what we have seen with our own eyes, what we have gazed upon, and what we have embraced with our own hands," and suggested that you take them and apply them to yourself at Mass. John met Jesus Christ in His physical Body. You cannot do that directly. You can do it only sacramentally and mystically. You can meet Him "under the appearances of . . ." But it is Jesus Christ whom you can see, hear, taste and touch. You can know Him whom you meet. You will love Him if you do meet Him; and meet Him you should in Mass; for Mass is an "encounter with God."

Now note that I am not suggesting that you will have a mystical experience in the strict, technical, limited sense of that term; an experience such as Teresa of Avila, John of the Cross, and other *bona fide* mystics describe and have experienced. That is a special grace from God. That is infused contemplation in the strict sense of the term. But you must come to the realization that the Reality that they experienced is a Reality, an ontological Reality, *in your own soul* this moment if you are in the state of grace. Therefore, there should be a psychological awareness of this Reality to some degree. And there will be if you think theologically.

Pause here long enough to ask yourself if there is any other way to think about reality except theologically. We are because God is. We find truth when we find God — and we find God every time we find truth. We live because the living God is the God of the living. Mass is the Reality of all realities, because Mass is Jesus Christ, and Jesus Christ is Mass. Mass is AGAPE — Love — and AGAPE is at the heart of all being.

That is put in by way of parenthesis because, today, there are those who will condemn with a phrase things that cannot be condemned, and by a phrase that should never be used to condemn. "Theologizing" is one such condemnatory term. Turn it back on those would-be thinkers by showing them how to think.

To face reality fully, we readily admit we are dealing with the supernatural; and the supernatural, in itself, is not the immediate object of awareness. We can know it only through faith. But a living faith, a lively and loving faith, will give anyone some sort of intuition of the mysterious Reality that is going on at Mass. Not only there, but down in the depths of your own soul, thanks to grace. Yes, and in every ordinary act of faith. In each of these three realities there is an encounter with God — and with each Person of the Trinity. We link them here; for they are linked in Mass — and each is necessary for the psychological awareness we are striving to produce.

Mass is the *Mysterium Fidei*. It requires faith. But have you ever realized that an act of faith is really an act of love — and that every act of love is, basically, an act of faith? For, if you will analyze it closely you will find that, ultimately, you do not believe a dogma of Faith, a revealed truth, or an article of the Creed. No. You believe a Person. That may sound like more of the modern "personalistic" approach. If it is that, it is so only because it is traditional. And I will say here something that may give you reassurance, or at least banish all fear about many of the things called "modern" in philosophy and theology: actually, they give us no new truth, but only new terms for traditional truths. The most you need grant them is a more vivid realization of what our forefathers always realized.

Look at this matter of faith. Tradition has always defined the act of faith as "an assent of the mind to revealed truth because of the authority of the one revealing." At times teachers have stressed "the assent of the mind"; at other times they have stressed "the revealed truth"; at still others the accent has been on "the authority of the one revealing." But do you not see that every assent of the mind is, ultimately, an act of trust in the *person* who does the revealing? Why do we believe that Jesus Christ is in Mass? Ultimately, because Jesus Christ said so, and we trust Jesus Christ; and in that trust we love the Second Person of the Blessed Trinity. Hence, faith is an "encounter with God." It is looking into the eyes of Jesus Christ, and saying: "I believe *YOU*."

But before any of us could ever do that there had to exist, in the ontological order, another "encounter with God"; that of grace

— Actual and Sanctifying. Theologians of yesterday, as well as of today, have always taught that grace effects an ontological transformation of the soul. By sanctifying grace you and I were elevated above the natural and given a share in the very Life of God. Thus there was established a new relationship between us and each of the Persons of the Trinity who then came to dwell within us. That spells "encounter with God." The "encounter" was actual from the first moment of the infusion of grace; for, from that moment, in the ontological order, the Triune God dwelt within us. It was a meeting of Persons — and a union of those who are opposed. But it was only in the ontological order; for, as St. Thomas Aquinas taught so lucidly, the Three Persons dwell within us as objects of knowledge and love, by virtue of sanctifying grace, *without* any particular acts of knowledge and love (L, 43, 3). That means that there is no necessary psychological awareness of the indwelling of the Three Persons. But there will be if you think theologically when offering Mass.

Mass is a Sacrifice. How do we know that? By the knowledge given by faith. We believe Jesus Christ. But how is it that we believe Him? The real answer to that is: "Because God has first loved us" (1 Jn 4:10). God gave us the grace to believe. It was a gift — and, because a gift, it had to be received by us. So you see the "encounter" that took place before Mass — and the "encounter" that takes place in Mass. Ontologically, there can be no question as to the Reality. Psychologically — that is up to us; for the supernatural life is a cooperative affair. It is Christ coming to us, knocking at the door of our hearts — and waiting for us to *invite* Him in.

Never is that more true than at Mass. We have knowledge of Christ's Presence in Mass. But we do not advert sufficiently to the actuality that Presence means *Person*. We need to enliven our act of faith in *HIS* Presence; make it an existential answer — to use more modern terminology (but to say nothing new) — to the dialogue of grace He initiated and continues. Realize, even if it be only in a hazy manner, that *HE* is there; then you will realize both Presence and Person. Then there will be a meeting, a new intentional union, thanks to a loving knowledge of Him. Thus every Mass will be a new contact with your Beloved; and, analogously, to every new contact with a human whom you know and love, there will be an increase in both your love and knowledge of your God.

Look at that analogy and spell it out. The more you love a person, the more you come to know him or her. Not what he or she is, but *who* he or she are. You can know a lot *about* a person without ever meeting him. But it is only by meeting him that you come to know him as a person; for a relationship is set up, a living relationship, and a conscious living out of the popular, if not overpopular, "I-Thou" relationship. There is actually that mutual knowledge and love which we have seen unites and opposes two persons.

Please do not think that I have suddenly gone "high hat" with all this modern terminology. It is only used to show you that there is nothing "old hat" about this way I show you of getting more out of Mass and becoming holier and holier through Mass.

Continual meeting with a human being deepens our knowledge of him as a person. We get clearer and deeper insight into that center which sustains his whole character, and thus come to know *who* he is better and better; not simply what he is. So it is with Christ. The more we meet Him in Mass, and meet Him as a Person, the more we come to know just *who* He is. We soon see that He *is* "our refuge and our strength" as David so often sang of old; and that upon Him we can rest our weakness as mortals as well as our soaring aspirations to immortality. We come to know Him as Love, and grow in our love of Him as the Truth, the Way, and the Life.

But never forget that Jesus is a divine Person. Hence, do not expect complete and exhaustive knowledge of Him as a Person. For, even with humans, the heart of his or her personality is always, and ever will remain, a mystery. How much more so that of a Person who is divine. Yet, just as man and wife grow in love, and come to mean more and more to one another from constant association, so will Christ come to mean more and more to us, the more we meet Him. Love will give us deeper and deeper insights; it will never give us complete knowledge, even in heaven. But Mass can be the closest thing to heaven while we are still on earth, if we will but make it the Reality it is; for it is Love.

Speaking of heaven reminds me that another very popular word in today's trends is "eschatological." It may appear a strange word to you, but what it actually describes is anything but strange. It tells of those things of which you are made continually conscious by that peculiar combination of paradoxical realities within you that we mentioned above: the uncertainties of your mortal existence and the utter, unchallengeable certitude of your immortality. "Eschatological" means the doctrine of "the last things": death, judgment, heaven, and hell. Those four center around Christ Jesus; for death is but the coming of Christ for each of us; then comes judgment by Christ; followed by either unending union with Him in loving knowledge and knowing love, or separation from Him for all eternity. Every Mass is "eschatological" inasmuch as every Mass is a "coming of Christ." In fact, in Paul's account of the institution of Holy Eucharist as Sacrifice and Sacrament, we find the words: "In reality, every time you eat this bread and drink the chalice of the Lord, you proclaim the Lord's death *until he comes*" (1 Cor 11:26).

As you see, that is to connect Mass with the final coming of Christ. For on the night He instituted this "memorial" — which was to be a living memorial — Christ was keenly conscious of the fact that on the morrow He would die. He also knew that one day He would return. He told us that Himself. He said it would be sudden. "As the lightning starts in the east and blazes its way to the west, so it will be with the advent of the Son of Man. . . . But regarding that day and hour, no one knows, not even the angels in Heaven, nor yet the Son, but only the Father" (Mt 24:27, 36). So, for the period between His going on the morrow and His final coming, Christ gave us Mass as a "memorial," as His sacramental coming every day to remind us of that final coming when "the sign of the Son of Man will appear in the sky," and He will be seen "riding the clouds overhead with great might and majesty" (Mt 24:30).

Mass, then, in its eschatological relation, should comfort us, and give us assurance that this world of ours will not perish by any "accident" produced by the folly of man. Christ has prophesied that He will put an end to it on that day and in that hour, "which the Father has fixed by his own authority" (Acts 1:7). It will then be that Christ will appear as Judge. But in Mass He comes as Food and Drink; as Lover with total gift of Self; one might say as Reward.

Mass, then, is a reminder not only of Christ's human end, but of our own end, and the end of time. It shows us Reality. It shows us that we are living ever in suspense; for the sudden, surprising, lightninglike coming of Christ is always a possibility of the next moment. At any hour Christ may come to judge the world. That is one of the Realities Mass should bring before us as we meet Christ in His Holy Sacrifice. And that Reality gives us JOY. For, while we know not what today will hold, let alone tomorrow; while we know not but what eternity may begin tomorrow or even today; we are sure that we are now meeting Christ — in Person — and all is well. That fact tells us that whatever comes after Mass this day, or any day, will also be well; for it will be of His making. With these truths before us, how foolish we would be not to make every Mass "eschatological."

For two loving and most loved friends of mine Mass was one day the end — eschatological in the sense that it was their definitive meeting with Christ as Judge, and as I have reason to hope, as Reward. One, a doctor, met Christ just as he was about to start for the Communion rail. The other, a priest, met Him just as he took the chalice, after vesting, and headed for the altar to celebrate Mass. Today's Mass could be "eschatological" in that sense for you — for me. . . .

One day I will celebrate my last Mass. Today could be that day.

One day you will offer your last Mass. That day could be tomorrow — it could also be today. See how uncertain we are. We cannot promise ourselves the next breath or heartbeat. But see how certain we are that Christ loves us: He offers Himself to us every day as Food and Drink, and, as I said above, as Lover offering His complete Self as total Gift. In very truth, He comes in every Mass as Reward. Why not look on His coming to take us in death in the same light? He will "come like a thief." He has promised us that. But it will only be to steal us away to the everlasting embrace of love we call heaven, if we make Mass our life and our life Mass. In every Mass He comes to give Himself to us entirely, to meet us face to face, to offer us "in Himself" to the Father. That is Mass. That is Love. That is the "wondrous exchange." That is Reality. That is "encounter with God."

CHAPTER FIVE

EPHPHATA

"Taste and see . . ."

This May morning I watched day break over the distant knobs. It was not only visual beauty; it was melody as well. More; it was dramatic revelation. The whole majestic sweep of the eastern skyline was in motion. As the deep red in the blue bosom of the dawn lifted itself, it paled to a lovelier rose, delicately rimmed with saffron, yellow, and light gold. Then, in slow, serene sovereignty, came the sun. As the May mists lifted from the fresh green of the fields and drifted toward the sun, they looked like vast, thin clouds of incense. It seemed that Nature was adoring. Soon I found myself softly declaiming the opening lines of Thompson's "Orient Ode":

> Lo, in the sanctuaried East
> Day, a dedicated priest
> In all his robes pontifical exprest,
> Lifteth slowly, lifteth sweetly
> From out its Orient tabernacle drawn
> Yon orbed sacrament confest
> Which sprinkles benediction through the dawn.

Who would not pity the man who had eyes to look upon this beauty-drenched world, yet see it not?

Then, as song burst from awakened robin, bobwhite, songsparrow, and cardinal, with the chatter of countless purple grackle in the high trees of the lane and the occasional scold of some swooping bluejay as background, I felt sorry for city dwellers who could not see and hear all that I was taking in, as well as for those in the country who were still asleep and missing all this blazing glory of God and soft melody over the world of men.

But then, as I thought of the work ahead of me this day on this book, I realized there is a sorrier plight than that of those who miss the magnificence of dawn. It is that of those who miss the Reality in Mass. They have eyes and see not; ears, yet do not hear; tongue, yet never savor. They are blinder far than was blind Bartimeus that memorable morning as he sat by the road to Jericho begging. For Jesus is nearer them at Mass than He was to Bartimeus. Moreover, Jesus is passing by. Yet they do not call out as did the blind man: "Jesus, Son of David, take pity on me." Let them do that but once, with sincerity and faith, and what happened to that beggar son of Timeus will happen to them. Jesus will say: "Your faith has cured you" (Mk 10:52).

Faith not only gives vision, it gives acute hearing, and the ability to savor delicately and with delight. But faith does not work automatically. We have to "stir it up," set it in motion.

There are those who may think this directive to see, hear, taste, and touch God in Mass something a bit too materialistic, too sense-involving, and on too low a level for the high spirituality that should be ours when encountering God in the supreme act of worship. These will have read or heard of that kind of contemplation which gives contact with "naked" truth, a direct "touching" of the essence of God in what is called the "dark night" of the senses, and even of the spirit, a nonconceptual awareness of God's presence within one. These will tell you that far from using our exterior senses, such as those of sight, hearing, taste, and touch, we should desist from using even our interior senses, our imagination, and even those finite ideas that are bound up with this world. They may even cite John of the Cross, the Doctor *par excellence* of Mysticism.

You need not argue with them. Allow them their way. But do not abandon this way! For if they demand authority for this kind of contemplation you will be far from bankrupt. You have St.

Bernard of Clairvaux to cite; you have St. Francis of Assisi to call
upon; and above all you have St. Ignatius of Loyola to sustain
you. These masters of Mysticism teach you the concrete type of
contemplation, tell you to use your imagination to the utmost, and
even your five external senses with all the sensitivity you can summon. These saints will have you use all the vivid images and clear
concepts that come from the Gospels, and have you very conscious
of the full sweep of the historical course of salvation. These in-
timates with God will have you ever mindful not only that the Son
of God took flesh, became man in the truest sense of humanness,
but that He is still living in that flesh — glorified, of course, by
the Resurrection. They will not have you looking at the "historical
Christ" but will bring you into closest possible personal contact
with the Incarnate Word of God who is your contemporary; in
whom you "live, and move, and have your being."

Again and again in his *Exercises* St. Ignatius tells you to "smell
and savor by scent, to taste the infinite perfume and sweetness of
the Divinity." That is no mere matter of imagination, he is urging
you toward. It is faith he is telling you to stir up and employ.
Faith gives vision — and more than vision; it spiritualizes all our
senses. Let us but recall that we are members of that Mystical
Body whose Head is the glorified Jesus Christ. Hence, we who have
died with Him, as St. Paul teaches, have also risen with Him, and
already, while in this life, have something of the glorification of
His senses in our own. Our senses have been spiritualized by grace,
by the indwelling of the Trinity, by a share in the very life of the
Godhead. Because we are "in Christ Jesus," we can look and see
Jesus Christ where He is; we can listen to Him and actually hear
what He says; we can do precisely what St. Ignatius suggests: we
can "smell and savor by scent, even taste the infinite perfume and
sweetness of our God."

That is no new directive. David, that "man after God's own
heart," urged all to "taste and see that the Lord is sweet" (Ps
33:91). St. Peter repeated it in that famous first letter we have
already cited: "As newborn babes long for the unadulterated

spiritual milk, so that you may grow up to salvation in the Lord. You have already *tasted* how sweet he is" (1 Pt 2:3). St. Paul also tells of those "who have relished the heavenly gift . . . who have *relished the sweetness* of God's word" (Heb 6:4).

Were I to stand in choir in Gethsemani's basilica and see nothing in my fellow monks assembled there for conventual Mass but a gathering of men; were I to listen to the subdeacon sing the Epistle and to the deacon as he sang the Gospel, and hear nothing more than men singing more or less melodiously; were I to watch the celebrant go through all the rubrics of Mass and observe the students as they received Holy Communion in that Mass, yet see nothing more than men, I would be blinder than any Bartimeus, deafer and more mute than any deaf and dumb man brought before Christ while He was in Palestine; I would be deader far than the widow of Naim's son, Jairus' little daughter, or even Lazarus who was four days in the grave and already corrupting when Jesus came to Bethany and the sorrowing sisters, Martha and Mary. The same will be true of you if ever you are in Church for Christ's all-holy Sacrifice and do not see, hear, taste, and touch the Christ of God and the Jesus of men.

At our Baptism, Christ, who was the real minister, as St. Augustine so lucidly taught, did for us precisely what He did that day in the "heart of the Decapolis" when the "people brought him one who was deaf and who spoke but imperfectly." Jesus took this man "away from the crowd, to be alone with him." Then He "put his fingers into the man's ears, and, with his own spittle, touched the man's tongue. He then looked up to heaven, sighed, and said to him: *'Ephphata,'* which means 'Open'" (Mk 7:32–37). Christ opened our eyes, unstopped our ears, loosed our tongues, rendered keen our sense of smell, and made highly sensitive our widespread tactile faculty. His *Ephphata* was effective. But it was left to our own free will whether we would further develop this spiritual acuity, or let it dull from disuse. God has tremendous respect for our liberty. In last analysis that may be but divine Self-respect; for it may be that there, in our free wills, is

the image and likeness of God. At any rate, we can say of Christ
what those in the "heart of the Decapolis" said of Him that day
He first said *Ephphata;* we can say: "Everything he has done is
wonderful! He gives hearing to the deaf . . ." (Mk 7:37).

This morning I offered the daily Mass for the departed. If I
heard only my own voice as I read the Epistle, which is taken from
St. John's Apocalypse, and found nothing personal in the lines
about "Blessed are the dead who die in the Lord . . . they are
to have rest from their toils, for their deeds accompany them"
(Ap 14:13); if I then went on to the Gospel and heard no other
voice than my own as I read: "He who eats my flesh and drinks
my blood is in possession of eternal life; and I will raise him up
from the dead on the last day" (Jn 6:54), Christ's *Ephphata* at
my Baptism was a wasted word. But, actually, I hardly heard my
own voice at all. I heard God the Holy Spirit speaking in the
Epistle — and He was talking to me personally, and very directly.
In the Gospel I heard the voice of Jesus Christ. He was not at
Capharnaum speaking to the crowds. He was in Gethsemani speaking to me. He was promising me eternal life and the resurrection
of my body. He was setting my soul singing *O Sacrum Convivium*
— that hymn by St. Thomas Aquinas which tells how in Holy
Communion I banquet on the holiness of God, receive Jesus
Christ, renew the memory of His Passion, have my soul filled to
the overflowing with grace, and am given solemn pledge of my
own future glory. I was listening for Christ's voice in my Mass.
I heard it with bell-like clarity. God spoke to me in Mass today
just as He speaks in Mass every day. So I say *Ephphata* — "Open
your ears" to the voice of Jesus Christ when at Mass.

Years ago in southern Germany there was a beautiful custom
which alerted all to reality. As the priest in a low Mass, or the
deacon in a sung Mass, moved over to read or sing the Gospel,
the people would cry out: "Behold, the Lord cometh!" Nowadays,
here in America, you have the same reality brought home to you,
if you are alert. For when the priest says or sings *Dominus
vobiscum* before he begins the Gospel, you should be so alert to

reality that you will say with your whole being: "Indeed, the Lord is with us — in Person. And He is about to speak to us personally and directly." For when the Gospel is read or sung it is no mere historical narration that is given to you; it is the contemporary Christ talking to you about contemporary issues; He is speaking to you as directly and as personally as He ever spoke to the Jews of old. *Ephphata* — "Open your ears" and hear Jesus Christ; the Word of God is giving you God's own words.

The word of God! The power it conjures up is that of creative omnipotence; for the first word of God we know of having been spoken is *Fiat* — it brought the universe into being. David was well aware of this and sang in one of his Psalms: "The word of God rings true, and all his works prove his fidelity. A word of God has made the firmament; a breath of his mouth, the starry hosts. . . . May all the earth revere the Lord; may all the world's inhabitants fear him! He spoke the word, and they were made; he uttered the command, they came to be!" (Ps 32:4–9.) The word of God brought you and me into being. The Word of God leads us on the way of life: "Your word — it is a lamp to guide my feet, a light to show my path" (Ps 118:105).

The word of God! We hear it in every Mass. Not only does the Living Word speak to us, but He speaks words that are life-giving. "Man does not live by bread alone; but by every word coming from the lips of God" (Mt 4:4). Those lips move every morning; they move in every Mass. And, as St. Paul tells us, "The word God speaks is living and effective . . ." (Heb 4:12). But those living words can be rendered dead, utterly ineffective if we do not implement what Christ effected in us by His *Ephphata* at Baptism. We must open our ears, not only to listen, but to actually hear. Then the words of Christ in Mass will be what St. Paul said they are meant to be, and what God wants them to be: life-giving.

You have heard the God-Man explain one of His own parables: that of the Sower and His seed. At Mass Christ is the Sower, and He is still sowing His seed; for, as He explained in the long, long ago: "The 'seed' is God's message" (Lk 8:11). You hear that

message in the Epistle and the Gospel. Your soul is the ground
into which Christ's "seed" falls. What is the nature of your soil?
Is it hard like that "close to the footpath"? Is it "stony ground"?
Have you allowed "thorns" to grow up in it? Or is it "the right
kind of soil" where the "seed" "sprouts and bears fruit a hundredfold"? It can be that kind if you will listen and hear. . . .

Test yourself. Could you tell me what it was that Christ said
to you this morning in Mass during the Epistle and the Gospel?
Only last Sunday (the Fifth after Easter) He spoke of "religious
practice pure and undefiled." Did you hear Him? He said it was
"to care for orphans and widows in their affliction, and to keep
oneself from being tainted by the world" (Jas 1:27). Had you been
as wise as was Mary Immaculate, you would have taken those
words into your very heart and pondered them there. You would
have heard Christ saying: "Meekly embrace the teaching planted
within you; it has the power to save your souls. Carry it into
action; do not be a mere listener. Otherwise you deceive yourselves" (Jas 1:21, 22).

If you will but open your ears which have already been opened
by God, you will never again have to lament your tiny garner
from Mass, nor wonder if you are becoming more holy through the
Holy Sacrifice; for you will become "doers of the word, and not
hearers only." Then you will come to have a foretaste of heaven;
for He who speaks to you is faithful, and one day He said:
"*Blessed* are they who hear the word of God and keep it" (Lk
11:28). Yes, you can taste beatitude long before eternal beatitude
has begun.

Listen to the word of God and hear Him; for "he who is sprung
from God gives ear to God's message" (Jn 8:48) and "all Scripture
is inspired by God and useful for teaching, for reproving, for
correcting, for instructing in holiness, that the man of God may be
perfect, fully equipped for every good deed" (2 Tim 3:16). Since
holiness is the ultimate of your life, you will learn how to attain to
that ultimate if you but listen to your God in Mass. He tells
you how.

As Christ ends His speaking in the Epistle, lively gratitude takes voice and says: "Thanks be to God!" When He ends His directive on life and living through His Gospel, gratitude again finds voice and says: "Praise be to Thee, O Christ!" Then comes the reverent kissing of the text.

If you will use the eyes God gave you through His *Ephphata* you will see Christ kissing Christ in every holy kiss that is given during Mass. A kiss is a sign. In Mass it is always a sacred sign, a sign of love. As Mass begins, the celebrant kisses the altar. It is a kiss of greeting. As he impresses it on the altar, which is a symbol of Christ, the priest prays that the Lord will forgive him all his sins. As he kisses the book at the end of the Gospel with a kiss of gratitude, he prays again that "his sins may be blotted out." This sacred sign, then, is sanctifying; it is a sacramental. When imparted with reverent sincerity it effects what every other sacramental can effect: the removal of venial sin.

You would kiss the Holy Shroud of Turin, I am sure. You kiss the cross often. A relic of the true Cross you would kiss with deep reverence. Then why not kiss the Gospels with like reverence? They are the words of God. The kiss you imprint can be meant for the Living Word, and you can be saying in your soul what the singer of the Song of Songs rendered so articulate by crying: "The voice I love! . . . I can hear my true love calling to me. . . . Show me thy face, let me but hear thy voice, that voice sweet as thy face is fair" (Ct 2:8–14). You can go further and have your heart begging for what this singer begged in her opening lines: "a kiss from His lips!" — for in Mass you not only see Christ and hear Him, you can touch Him as well.

St. Bernard of Clairvaux is generally held to have been the author of the hymn *Jesu dulcis memoria,* in which it is said: "Jesus, the very thought of Thee gives true joy to my heart, but surpassing all honey and all honied sweetness is Thy presence. Nothing sweeter can be sung, nothing pleasanter can be heard, nothing lovelier can be thought than Thy name. How good Thou art to those that seek Thee! But what to those that find! No tongue can tell, nor written word express it: only he who has had the experience can tell what it means to love Thee."

If Bernard could use his spiritualized senses on the mere thought of the name Jesus and of His presence, what can you not do with senses similarly spiritualized when you can not only think of Christ but actually touch Him; have Him on your tongue; take Him entirely — Body, Blood, Soul, Divinity — into your own body and blood. Touch . . . !

When Christ was at Capharnaum one day, surrounded by a huge crowd, an official of the Synagogue pressed his way through that throng, threw Himself at Jesus' feet, and pleaded with Him to come and restore life to his young daughter who had just died. Christ immediately set out with Jairus — for that was the man's name — "accompanied by so large a crowd that they were all but smothering him" (Mk 5:24).

Into that throng there came a woman who had spent her entire fortune on doctors; but instead of getting relief and a cure, she had gone from bad to worse. Despite the throng, she managed to get close enough to Jesus to touch His garment. Instantly she was cured. At the same instant Jesus stopped and asked: "Who is it that touched my garments?" St. Mark tells us that the disciples were so surprised at this question that they all but rebuked Christ, saying: "You see the crowd is all but smothering you, and you ask: 'Who has touched me?'" But Mark also tells us that Jesus was conscious that His healing power had been active. What insight that gives us into the healing power of Jesus Christ! His very garments were alive with it. The incident also gives us insight into the faith of this poor woman; for she had kept saying to herself: "If I but touch his garment I shall be healed."

This was one of the strangest miracles ever wrought by Christ. All the others — be they the calming of tempests, the curing of cripples, lepers, or the palsied, the giving of sight to the blind, hearing to the deaf, or even raising the dead to life — were done deliberately. On every such occasion Jesus was master of the situation and did what He willed. At Capharnaum, however, it would seem that the miracle was performed indeliberately. Something flowed out of Him. Something seemed to have been taken from Him in spite of Himself. When the woman came forward and told her story, Christ had only eulogy and love for her because of her lively faith. "Daughter, your faith has cured you. Go home and be at peace" (Mk 5:34).

"If I can but touch . . ." What did she have on which to base her faith? Not two full years of His wonder-working. We have had two thousand. She had seen Him. She had heard Him. We cannot doubt but that she was singularly blessed by God, else she would never have believed as she did. But she never had what you and I have: the elevation of our entire being by Baptism, the spiritualization of our senses by the same Sacrament, and the gift of a share in the very life of God. She was not a member of His Mystical Body. Yet she believed with a belief that moved the Son of God to eulogy. "If I but touch his garment, I shall be well." You can touch more than His garment. You can touch His whole Body. You can receive His whole Self. You can be made completely well. For you can come as close to God as He is to Himself. And He wants this closeness!

It is possible that you may have envied Adam his opportunity to walk with God in the Garden of Paradise, as we read that he did "in the afternoon air." You may have even grown angry with Eve for having robbed you of a like opportunity by listening to the serpent and allowing herself to be deceived. But you need not. Nor need you sigh with empty regret for not having been called into existence during those days when Jesus Himself walked the earth. For our world of the present moment, despite the savage barbarity prevalent within it, teems not only with more possibilities for intimacy with God, but for greater intimacy. You can have personal possession of much more divine life than Paradise ever knew. Granting that there are countless things in the present day that are to be grievously lamented and strenuously opposed, nevertheless we should be rejoicing that we live in the era after Christ; for the reality that rejoices the heart of man is that the re-creation brought about by the Incarnate Word of God surpasses far the original creation brought to climax by the production of Adam and Eve. It is in the re-creation that we live! Which is better: Adam as father or Christ as brother? to walk beside God in the afternoon air or take God within you in the morning?

Now that is not to blind ourselves to anything that resulted from the original fall of man. That is not to close our eyes to the fact that within each of us there are three concupiscences, seven capital sins, a darkened intellect and a weakened will. But it is meant to open our eyes to the greater fact that our intellects have been enlightened, our wills strengthened, theological and moral Virtues infused, Gifts given, and on top of all that there is the opportunity to be filled with God whom we can see, hear, taste, touch, and take completely into ourselves.

"If I but touch his garment . . ." O woman, great was your faith, and great its reward. But how much greater should ours be! You did touch His garment and were made whole. We can eat His Flesh, drink His Blood — and that not only once in a lifetime, but every day of the year. Pray for us, woman of the issue of blood; pray that we sharpen our sense of wonder and our realization of our oneness with Christ Jesus in His Mystical Body; pray that we quicken our gratitude for the largesse of God which allows us a daily reception of His physical Body. Ask the Christ who made you whole, to awaken us to the glory that is ours in our ability to touch Him daily.

No one need tell you that you do not touch God immediately and directly. You recognize the fact that it is only the species of Bread and Wine that you so touch. But what is being stressed here is that under those species it is the living God you *do* touch as you take Him into your body and being. It is the same Jesus Christ who said to the Magdalen the first Easter morn: "Do not hold me . . ." (Jn 20:17) and one week later said to Thomas: "Let me have your finger; put it here, and look at my hands. Now let me have your hand, and lay it into my side" (Jn 20:27). The Magdalen and Thomas really touched the risen Christ. So do you

— just as really, though not as directly. Yet, while you need not probe with your fingers, nor prove with your hands, you do need to exclaim as did St. Thomas: "My Master, and my God!" For in Holy Communion you do more than Thomas did that Sunday night in the Cenacle; you take those nail-pierced hands and that lance-wounded side into your very own body! And you are "blessed" — you should savor beatitude. For this same risen Jesus, on this very same occasion, said to Thomas: "*Blessed* are those who have not seen and yet believe" (Jn 20:29). Christ was talking about you.

Holy Communion climaxes and completes this Act of Love called Mass; for it gives the ultimate in that "wondrous exchange."

We exchange words with God: for after our words in the Introit, Kyrie, Gloria and Oration, God gives us His words in the Epistle and Gospel.

We exchange sight and presence with God; for after seeing Him in the people, the priest and ourselves, God looks out at us present, and sees us from under the appearances of Wheat and Wine.

Then we exchange our very selves; for the wheat, wine, and water we give are symbols of the totality of our being that we wish to give to God, and He — He offers us His humanity and divinity.

How incomplete our Act of Love called Mass would be, if we failed to touch God in Holy Communion. Love wants union; living union and union for life. Could any lovers have greater union, more living union, expressly for life, than that offered us by God in the Holy Sacrifice of Mass?

Should you have failed with any frequency to take God into the complete embrace of love offered in Holy Communion, you have, to some extent, at least, a very direct answer to the query about getting so little out of Mass and not becoming holier through Mass; for the prayer of the celebrant in the Canon points out this truth for us. He bends low and humbly asks God "that as many of us who, by participation at this altar, shall receive the most sacred Body and Blood of Thy Son may be filled with every heavenly blessing and grace. Through the same Christ our Lord."

How intimate is the touch God allows! The Communion prayer often said in the Mass in honor of our Lady runs: "Blessed is the womb of the Virgin Mary, which bore the Son of the Eternal Father." As you go back from the Communion rail, you bear in your body that same Son of that same Eternal Father! Are you not blessed at that moment with the blessedness Mary knew in her Maternity? True, you are bearing Him in a different manner, and for a different purpose; but you are bearing Him!

Do you know precisely for what purpose you are bearing Him? You will know if you but try to fathom the reason why God offers Himself to you "under the appearances" of Bread and Wine. Briefly, it is to satisfy the basic hunger and thirst of your being. David described you to the life when he cried: "O God, my God you are! With anxious heart I look for you! My soul, my flesh — they thirst, they yearn for you, like dried-up, thirsting, waterless soil" (Ps 62:1).* That is you. That is the thirst of your being. You are a desert thirst for God. You are a gnawing, pain-filled hunger for Him. So Christ says to you: "My flesh is real food, and my blood real drink . . . he who eats me will have life because of me" (Jn 6:57). He also says: "I tell you the plain truth: unless you eat the flesh of the Son of Man and drink his blood, you have no life in you" (Jn 6:53).

How God loves you! He becomes your Food and Drink — that you may live!

Think a little further. Bread is food. For it men never lose their taste. It is life-giving, life-sustaining. Christ is our Living Bread — the Food of our souls. By giving Himself as Bread, He gives us our real life, and sustains it; for instead of assimilating this Bread into ourselves, we are assimilated into It — and become ever more who we are: Christ.

Wine is drink, but it is more than drink; more than plain water that quenches the thirst. Wine exhilarates. God Himself told us so through Sirach: "Wine was created from the beginning to make

---

* Kleist-Lynan, *The Psalms in Rythmic Prose*. Bruce, 1954.

men joyful" (31:35). Christ gives us Himself under the guise of wine. He wants to more than quench our thirst. He wants to make us joy-filled. He would have us happy with His own happiness, which comes from His own holiness. Ignatius of Loyola understood this, and prayed as we should ever pray: *Sanguis Christi, inebria me!* — "Blood of Christ, inebriate me!" Someone has described truly religious men as men who were "drunk with God."

Now you see why God chose such essential signs. He would signify clearly His purpose in giving Himself to you. He comes to give life and make you happy. This Bread gives the only true life. This Wine gives the only joy that is true.

Sacraments effect what they signify. This Sacrament signifies and effects your sanctification. That is really why you live: to be filled with God, who alone is Sanctity. Look at the signs of the Eucharistic Sacrament and see how they signify the cause, the essence, the ultimate goal of your sanctification. The *cause* of your sanctification is the Passion, Death, Resurrection, and Ascension of Jesus Christ. You have all four in Mass. The *essence* of your sanctification consists in your participating in God's own life. In Mass you have the living God who offers Himself to you precisely that you may participate in His life. The *ultimate goal* of your sanctification is eternal life with the eternal God, everlasting glory. Aquinas tells you that in this *Sacrum Convivium* — this sharing of life and living with God — you receive a *pignus futurae gloriae* — "a promise, a seed, of your future glory."

These signs, then, are not only commemorative of something past: Christ's Passion, Death, Resurrection, and Ascension; but are also demonstrative of something present: the life won by that Passion, Death, Resurrection, and Ascension — grace; finally, they are prophetic signs of your future: your glory with the God of Glory.

Touch God and live. Taste God and see that He is sweet! Do it by opening your God-opened being and receiving therein your God.

There is one more lesson to learn from these signs. By their very nature and all they signify these signs tell you why Holy

Eucharist is not like Baptism: to be received only once in a lifetime. Your hold on your human life is so fragile that you have to regain it, as it were, many times a day. That is why you take in food and drink. Your hold on the life of God within you is even more frail. The world with its vivid distractions and enticing attractions, the flesh with its demands that are often so imperious, the devil with his consummate wiliness, and, maybe above all three, your own selfishness, tend hourly to weaken your hold on your life in and love of God. You will hold that life fast and enflame that love to ever greater ardor if you will embrace God the way He wants to be embraced in Holy Communion — and do so daily; for daily you need this Food and Drink.

Life — ever more vigorous life — is the purpose of God's condescension in offering Himself for this embrace of love called Holy Communion. Therein you receive not only the living God, but the very God of life. He gives Himself precisely that you may have "more abundant life." That is why St. Augustine said: "Whoever wishes life, knows henceforth in whom he should live and from whom he must have life. Let him approach and believe. He must allow himself to be incorporated in order to be vivified. . . . Then he will live in God and for God."

But you can say even more. You can add that you will live for men as well. For the life you receive in Holy Communion is the Christ-life. But the living Christ is the Head of the Mystical Body. You are His member. Hence, when you receive Him, you not only nourish the God-life in your own person, but the God-life in every person who is a member of Christ's Mystical Body. The stronger you are spiritually, the holier you become with God's own holiness, and the more God-life you have within you, the stronger, holier, more filled with the life of God will be the Mystical Body of Christ. For just as in your human body each member affects every other member, because it is a unit, so, too, in Christ's Mystical Body which is just as much a unit and enjoys a sacred, sublime unity.

In Mass, then, Christ is truly loving Christ — and you are

helping Him do it. He is striving, as it were, to answer His own prayer, offered at His First Mass: "that all may be one." Love craves unity as avidly as love craves union. Christ's union with you in Holy Communion advances somewhat the unity of all His mystical members both among themselves and with Him. Rejoice, then, in your opportunity to love God and men as you wisely and truly love yourself in Mass and Holy Communion.

Love gives. Total love gives totally. But since love can exist only between persons, it is obvious that in all-out love it is the self, the whole self, that must be given. That is exactly what Christ gives in Mass. Hence it can be said with truth that all-powerful though He be, God cannot do any more than He does in Mass; all-wise though He be, He cannot devise anything wiser than Holy Mass; all-good though He be, He cannot desire anything better than Mass; all-holy though He be, He cannot present you with more holiness than He does in Mass; and all-loving though He is, He cannot love you more fully than He does in the Holy Sacrifice which culminates in that Sacred Banquet called Holy Communion.

But love is an "exchange." Hence, after seeing what God offers you in Mass, you must look to see what you can offer God in this same Act of Love.

In the Holy Sacrifice God grants you what are known as Love's Three Great Intimacies: those of sight, hearing, and touch. You see God. You hear God. You are granted love's most intimate embrace. But if Mass is to be that "wondrous exchange" you must be as liberal with God as He has been with you.

PART TWO

YOU ARE IN THE HANDS OF GOD

CHAPTER SIX

THIS IS HOW YOU LOOK IN THE EYES OF GOD

Love's First Intimacy

> *O wad some Pow'r the giftie gie us*
> *To see oursles as ithirs see us!*

Who has not said that — or at least felt like saying it? But does the image we create in the eyes and minds of others really count when ultimates are in the balance? Actually, the only concern that should be ours is how we look in the eyes of God. To know how He sees us requires no special new gift from above. All it demands is great honesty from below — from us. If we will summon all the humility possible — which is only another name for honesty — we will learn just how we look in the eyes of God — especially when at Mass.

God sees us as we are. For He is the all-seeing God. He looks on us — and finds us *very lovable.*

I hope that shocks you. I hope it produces so violent a reaction that you will be turned into a veritable torrent of questions, the central one of which will be: *Why should God love me?*

I'll tell you. I'll tell you exactly. I'll tell you truthfully. Ultimately, it is because God loves Himself. More proximately it is because God loves His only-begotten Son. Still more immediately it is because God is grateful — *to you.*

Now hold your judgment until we have thought this through.

When you are at Mass you can be in only one of two states. There is no third possibility. Either you are in the state of grace or you are in the state of sin. God sees you just as you are. He knows infallibly in just which state you stand. And, no matter which state He finds you in, He looks on you *with love*. For you are not only lovable, but actually, you have been and ever will be, so long as you are on earth, the special object of His love and loving.

You are the crown of God's visible creation; the final product of His diffusive love. And He, who is Love, made you to His own image and likeness. Looking upon you with all-seeing eyes, how could He find you other than lovable? Shakespeare was realistic and right when he had Hamlet exclaim: "What a piece of work is a man! How noble in reason! how infinite in faculty! in form, in moving how express and admirable! in action how like an angel! in apprehension how like a god!" You may want to remind me that Hamlet ended this soliloquy with the cry: "And yet, . . .what is this quintessence of dust?" If you do, I will remind you that one of the truest lines written in this mad century of ours runs: "Remember dust, that thou art splendor!" That is said without any reference to your future glory. That is said about you, as you stand in the present time; for you are splendor enough to be God's image and likeness. But after Baptism, and when at Mass, God sees you as truer and greater splendor; for then He sees you "in Him" who is called *Splendor Paternae Gloriae* — "The Splendor of the Father's Glory." Lovable, then, by creation, you have been made even more lovable by re-creation.

Of course you may be able to argue that all this would be true about you if you had retained your baptismal innocence and advanced from virtue to virtue, but as things are, you have often felt — and with reason — that "of all man's clotted clay the dingiest clot" was you. Well, for the sake of argument, suppose God looked down on you at Mass and found you in just such a state; what would you follow? You would have firmest reason for offering Mass with all the force of your being — and God would find you lovable in that offering; for then you would realize to the fullest the fundamental purpose of the Cenacle, the Cross, and the empty Tomb. Christ, you see, died for sinners. Mass is the living memorial of that Death; a memorial made present to give life, the glorious life won for sinners by the Son of God.

We often say that the God-Man died to glorify God. We are right. But we are just as right when we say that the God-Man died to glorify man. In fact there is no other way to glorification for any of us save through that God-Man who offers and is offered in Mass. St. Paul expressed it concisely when he said: "For our sakes God made sin of him who knew no sin, so that in him we might become God's holiness" (2 Cor 5:21). Look long at those first three monosyllables: "for our sakes." What can they mean but that God found you and me lovable long before we had any of His grace in us; lovable enough, even and especially when in our sins, to send His only Son "so that in him we might become God's holiness"? Consequently, when at Mass, even in the state of sin, God finds you lovable. And you should find Him and His Son so lovable that your very state of sin should spur you on to more loving, more intimate, more grateful offering of His Sacrifice and yours — Mass.

Too many good people, in all sincerity, dwell on their "unworthiness" to offer Mass. What human being, what angel or archangel, what cherub or seraph could ever be worthy to offer God to God? No man is worthy. No man ever will be. No man ever need be. For the only One who is, or ever will be worthy, is the Principal Offerer in every Mass. Christ offers Christ — and offers Him in expiation. There is the truth that heartens us all. We offer Mass "through Christ, with Christ, and in Christ," not because we are worthy, but precisely because we are unworthy. We offer the "Lamb of God who takes away the sins of the world." And, as the Council of Trent taught, "the Lord, appeased by the oblation thereof, and granting the grace and gift of penitence, forgives even heinous crimes and sins" (Sess. XXII, cap. 2). That does not mean that our mortal sins are forgiven directly at Mass. It only means that at Mass God finds us lovable enough to grant us, because of the offering of Mass, grace enough to bring us to our supernatural senses and send us to His Sacrament of Penance with the proper dispositions.

Mass is not Passion only, it is Resurrection as well. God, looking on any sinner, looks on him with love because He sees in his soul Christ ready for the glory of Resurrection. It may well be that God is waiting for this Act of Love — this Mass — to make your soul Easter!

When Jesus Christ came to the banks of the River Jordan and insisted that John the Baptist baptize Him, the heavens opened, the Holy Spirit descended in the form of a dove, and the voice of God the Father was heard saying: "This is my Son, the beloved, with whom I am well pleased" (Mt 3:17). In that Son, who is God's Beloved, you were incorporated at your Baptism. But Head and members of this Mystical Body form but one Mystic Person — the Whole Christ. Therefore, it is "in Christ Jesus," whom the Father loves, that the Father sees you at Mass. Could He see you otherwise than as lovable?

But it is not as member only that God sees you, it is as priest as well. Therefore, God sees you as one His Son actually *needs*. That is a strange-sounding thing to say. But it is actual truth. God needs you. God needs you if there is to rise from this earth of ours that Sacrifice which alone can glorify God. Since, then, you satisfy a need of His only Son, God looks on you with grateful love.

This one truth can change your whole life, show you how to get more and more out of Mass, and how to become ever holier through the Holy Sacrifice; for it tells you just how important you are to God. Calvary is over. Christ went through His Passion and died with the cry on His lips: "It is now completed" (Jn 19:20). "Father, into your hands I commit my spirit" (Lk 23:46). But Calvary is forever. For this same Christ who cried: "It is now completed" is He who commanded those in the Cenacle to "Do this as my memorial" (Lk 22:20). In other words, this One Priest of the New Testament wanted His One Sacrifice of the New Testament to be offered "from the rising of the sun even to the going down" (Mal 1:11). But how could that be were it not for you, for me, for the members of His Mystical Body? How vividly this presents the truth about Mass to each of us! Christ does not suffer again. Christ does not die again. But Christ does make His Suffering, Death, and Resurrection — His Sacrifice — present again in Mass. Here He is Priest just as He was there. Here is Victim just as He was there. But here His manner of offering is different from what it was there. There He offered with His own hands. Here He offers through your hands, through my hands, through the hands of all who are priests.

This is mystery, of course — deep, yet anything but dark. There is the blaze of God's glory about it; and it makes clear the blazing glory of man. Words may be wanting to describe this wonder, yet we can say with accuracy that Christ has given us His Sacrifice to be presented in sacramental form. Calvary of the past is made a present reality under signs that effect what they signify. The Body and Blood of Calvary's Victor — the glorified Christ — are made present on our altars under the sacramental signs of Bread and Wine. But before that glorified Victor can become present some man like myself, ordained by some bishop, must put himself at the disposal of Christ, give Him his breath, his hands, his mind, heart, will, and whole being, so that Christ can use him as His instrument, and, through him, say and do again what He said and did in the Cenacle: take bread, bless, break, and give saying: "Take and eat. This is My Body." Then, after blessing the wine, say: "Drink you. This is My Blood." Thus does Christ make Calvary, and all that Calvary connotes and embraces, a present Reality. Thus does He become present to us as Sacrifice and Sacrament. But let it be noted again, that to effect this marvel and mystery, he actually *needs* priests.

The Council of Trent made this as clear as it can be made by three all-important words: Mass is a *commemoration,* a *re-presentation,* and an *application.* It is a commemoration inasmuch as Calvary ended in what we call the year A.D. 33. It is a re-presentation inasmuch as Jesus Christ, the Victim and Victor of Calvary, is made present by transubstantiation in each particular place where an ordained priest consecrates bread and wine. It is an application inasmuch as the merits won by Jesus Christ on Calvary are poured out through Mass.

Studying those three all-important words we can see how one can dare to say that while the physical Christ *redeemed* it is the mystical Christ who *saves*. Redemption was accomplished when Christ cried out: "It is now completed." But salvation, as far as we are concerned as individuals, was only begun. The Fountain-head of all sanctification and salvation is Jesus Christ who is the same in Mass as on Calvary. St. Thomas Aquinas tells you that "it was through His triumph on the Cross that Jesus won power and dominion over Gentiles." But Pius XII adds: "By that same victory He increased that immense treasury of graces which, as He reigns gloriously in Heaven, He lavishes continually on His mortal members"; and He lavished them particularly through Mass (cf. *Mystici Corporis,* § 37).

Here, then, is why God the Father, God the Son, and God the Holy Spirit, look on you with special love: through you, with you, and in you, Christ, the Only Priest of the New Law, can offer His Sacrifice today for the same purpose He offered Himself on Calvary in the long, long ago — the glory of the Father and the salvation of men. He *needs* you as His coadjutor; and you have offered yourself to be such by your Baptism.

This is deep mystery. But do not think it is my personal doctrine. This marvelous and stimulating truth was taught publicly, officially, and universally by Pius XII in his magnificent encyclical on the Mystical Body. He said: "Because Christ the Head holds such an eminent position, one must not think that He does not *require* the Body's help. What Paul said of the human organism is to be applied likewise to this Mystical Body: 'The head cannot say to the feet: I have no need of you' — marvelous though it appear: *Christ requires His members.*" Then this saintly and learned Pontiff added: "This is not because He is indigent and weak, but rather because He has so willed it for the greater glory of His unspotted Spouse. Dying on the Cross He left His Church the immense treasury of the Redemption; toward this she contributed nothing. But when those graces come to be distributed, not only does He share this task of sanctification with His Church, but He wants it to be due, in a way, to her action" (*Mystici Corporis*, §§ 54, 55).

You well know what that action is at its highest point: the Act of Love called Mass. Pius XII left us in no doubt on this point, for he went on to say: "In this Act of Sacrifice through the hands of the priest, whose word alone has brought the Immaculate Lamb to be present on the altar, the Faithful themselves, with one desire and one prayer, offer it to the Eternal Father — the most acceptable victim of praise and propitiation for the Church's universal needs" (*Mystici Corporis*, § 97).

Mass will mean more to you if you will realize how much you are needed in Mass. Life itself will be more meaningful when you awake to the truth that your own sanctification and salvation, as well as that of many others, depends upon you and the way you use your priestly power. Men are saved by men — especially by the offering of Mass. What is more, the very efficacy of this all-powerful Sacrifice depends, in some degree, on your personal holiness. What a challenge that makes of life and holy living.

Mass, inasmuch as it is Christ's offering, is not only always perfectly acceptable to God, but is of infinite value as well. But, inasmuch as it is your offering and mine, and that of every other member of the Mystical Body, it is not always completely acceptable, and, consequently, not as valuable nor as effective as it could and should be. This fact can and should humiliate us. It also should serve as spur. We can limit the effectiveness of God's great Act of Love; we finite beings can set bounds to the veritable flood of God-life made possible by the Infinite Son of the Infinite Father. For the effectiveness of each and every Mass depends not only on the holiness of the entire Church offering it to Christ, but on the holiness of the individual priest who consecrates, as well as on the holiness of the faithful present who participate in the priesthood of Christ and who are here to offer God to God.

The learned and holy Maurice de la Taille, S.J., professor of

Theology at the Pontifical Gregorian University, a universally recognized authority on the Holy Sacrifice, author of the brilliant and profound *Mysterium Fidei,* wrote: "It is, then, of greatest importance that there should be in the Church many holy, many very holy persons. Devout people, men and women, who should be urged by every means to higher sanctity, so that *through them the value of our Masses be increased,* and the tireless voice of the Blood of Christ, crying from the earth, may ring with greater clearness and insistence in the ears of God. His Blood cries on the altars of the Church, but, since it cries through us, it follows that the warmer the heart, the purer the lips, the more clearly will its cry be heard at the Throne of God. Would you wish to know why for so many years after the first Pentecost the Gospel was so marvelously propagated; why there was so much sanctity amongst the Christian people; why such purity in heart and mind, such charity, the sum itself of all perfections? You will find the answer when you recall that in those times the Mother of God was still on earth giving her precious aid in all the Masses celebrated by the Church; and you will cease to wonder that never since has there been such expansion of Christianity, and such spiritual progress. For, apart from the first grace, which in respect to the Church corresponded to the Descent of the Holy Spirit, all other graces have, so to speak, to be purchased from God through its aid. These graces the Church earned then; these graces the Church earns now — in a smaller measure indeed, yet always in a measure worthy of God and sufficient for the elect. Its daily increase in worth and efficiency should be our earnest endeavor. May the offering of the Church, by increase in sanctity of her members, every day increase in worth and efficiency."*

God looks on you with love. That cannot be gainsaid. But now you see why that love-look of God can be filled with anxiety. His only Son *needs* you as mystical member and offering priest. What

---

* *The Mystery of Faith: Book 2, The Sacrifice of the Church.* Tr. from the French by Joseph Carroll and P. J. Dalton. New York: Sheed & Ward, 1950, p. 240.

is more, the efficacy of His Act of Love — Mass — depends on your degree of holiness. God looks on you with love — and there is pleading in His eyes. . . . His command: "Be holy . . ." is almost a prayer.

The saintly Francis Suarez, perhaps the most learned of all the learned Jesuit theologians, taught that "the holier priests are, the more beneficial to the faithful are their Sacrifices." True, he was thinking of priests who consecrate; but what he said concerning them can be said about you with equal truth: the holier you are, the more beneficial will every Mass be to God, to His only Son, to yourself, to the Mystical Body, and to all mankind. I put the beneficiaries in that order, for I would have you realize that at every Mass there issues from Christ a veritable torrent of grace which first strikes the celebrating priest, then saturates the servers, be they clerics or nonclerics, then goes out to engulf in love all you who are present and have offered this Mass, only to break out beyond you and bathe in its beneficial flow every member of the Mystical Body, and finally to lave all mankind. Who is there, with that fact before them, who would not labor day after day, and every hour in the day, to become more and more holy just that God and mankind would be better off? Who is there who would not strive to live in such a way that he or she can look up and say: "My God, I love You more today than I did yesterday; but not as much today as I will tomorrow — and all thanks to Mass!"

Become holier through Mass? — Certainly, if you live conscious of your priesthood. Realizing that you placed yourself "in Christ Jesus" in Mass every morning, you will take every happening of the day as He took every happening after His Gethsemani prayer: "Not my will, but Thine be done." You place yourself "in Christ Jesus" to do the will of God — not only in pleasant things, but especially in things that go against the grain. You can pray always as Christ did: "Let this chalice pass . . ." but never without adding ". . . nevertheless, not my will but Thine be done." Living conscious of your priesthood you will look upon every duty of your state in life, be it that of father, mother, husband, wife, sister, brother, single lay person or religious, as wheat and wine and water — to be offered in your Mass. You will finally come to see yourself as God sees you: as "Christ's wheat."

I borrowed that telling phrase from Ignatius of Antioch. He was Bishop of that early and important see when Trajan was emperor of Rome. Legend has it that Ignatius was the child Jesus took and placed before His disputing disciples and told them that unless they became as "this little child" they would not even enter the Kingdom of Heaven, let alone hold high places in that Kingdom. But, be that as it may, the historical facts are that Ignatius braved Trajan and fearlessly witnessed to Christ when that tyrant unleashed his bitter persecution of the early Christians. Trajan ordered the aged Bishop to be brought to Rome so that he would serve as a spectacle. As the ship carried him toward the Eternal City word reached Ignatius that a Christian, who was a cousin to the Emperor, was about to use his influence at Court and negotiate for the Bishop's liberation. Ignatius wrote a letter that stands in Christian literature as a monument. In it he set down that sentence which tells you, and me, and every Christian just what his vocation is. "I am *God's grain,*" wrote Ignatius, "and I am to be ground by the teeth of wild beasts so that I may be found to be *the pure bread of Christ.*"

You and I need not be "ground by the teeth of wild beasts," but we do need to become "the pure bread of Christ"; for we are indeed "God's grain." This truth is set like a jewel in the very center of Mass; for the prayer in the Canon, which follows immediately on the Consecration, sets forth the whole purpose of our lives as it says: "We offer unto Thy most excellent Majesty, of Thy gifts and presents, a pure Victim, a holy Victim, a spotless Victim." That, of course, refers to Christ who has just come in Person beneath the appearances of Bread and Wine; but you and I are "in Christ Jesus"; we are His members, and members and Head form one Mystic Person, the One who is offered in every Mass. How definite that makes the fact that Mass is not only His

Sacrifice, but ours as well. We are "God's grain — the wheat of Christ." We are His water as well. . . .

You already know that into each chalice of wine that is to be offered the celebrating priest must pour a few drops of water. In sign and symbol, that water is you. Read that sign, and see all that is symbolized. We who have been baptized are united to Jesus Christ in a community of life; in Mass we express this sublime mystery in an Act of Love that is rich in symbols and signs; one of the richest and most significant being this commingling of water with wine. In the middle of the third century St. Cyprian, who was then Bishop of Carthage, set it forth in eloquent terms: "Because Christ bore us all in Himself, because He bore even our sins, we see represented by the water all mankind, and by the wine the Blood of Christ. When the water is mixed with the wine in the chalice, the people are associated with Christ. This mingling of the water and wine is so intimate, their union in the Chalice of the Lord is so close, that they cannot be separated any more from each other. So it is with the Church. . . . Nothing can separate her from Christ, or prevent her from remaining united to Him in a love that is indissoluble. If the wine alone is offered, the Blood of Christ is made present without us; if the offering is made in water alone, the people are present without Christ. . . . But the people are never without Christ. Our souls must remain convinced of this inspiring certitude. We are never alone in making our offering: our offering is overshadowed by His, lost in the ocean of His oblation. This is the basis of our life in spite of our unworthiness. But, likewise, Christ is never without His people. He has never made His offering of Himself, He never will make it, without us. Here we touch what is most sacred in the Christian Mystery."

Here is the unfathomable mystery. Here is the humility of God. Here is love. Look at it: you can expiate even though the Christ has expiated fully; you can satisfy even though Christ has already satisfied superabundantly; you can merit today even though Christ merited fully, and for all, in the long, long ago; you can offer God to God even though Christ has not only already offered Himself, but has been accepted and made Eternal *Theotyte*. Think of it! You can help God who is Omnipotence, and help Him in the one work He long ago completed. That is what makes each dawn so desirable, and every day so valuable: you can help God. No wonder He looks on you *with love!*

CHAPTER SEVEN

THIS IS WHAT GOD HEARS FROM YOU — AT MASS

Love's Second Intimacy

One of the most comforting lines in Scripture is the tenth verse of the seventh Psalm, which runs: "Just God, thou art the searcher of the mind and heart."

How often do humans try to read our minds and see things there that never existed. How often do we try to express ourselves only to have our listeners hear things we have never said. Words often get warped as they pass from the lips of the speaker to the mind of the hearer, and things that were never said are heard, meanings that were never meant are given, intentions that were never even conceived are brought forth fully grown. But such can never be the case with our God who is that "Just God . . . searcher of the mind and heart."

That is most comforting; for prayer has been defined as the "lifting up of mind and heart to God." The Psalmist assures us that God is a Listener who hears, and hears aright; for He looks into the mind and heart of the one who prays. God listens as a lover; He hears every word that leaves the lips and all that is in the heart and can never find its way to the lips.

Many words are spoken in Mass. Each can be filled to the brimming-over with meaning. But, being such frail creatures, we know that there is such a thing as "lip service"; and we fear it not only among ourselves who are human, but even between ourselves and our God. We recall that it was He who told us about "lip service" in words that strike terror into any thinking man. Christ lashed out at the Scribes and Pharisees with that withering word: "Hypocrites!" and then went on to tell them just what a hypocrite is by saying: "Rightly has Isaias prophesied about you when he said: 'This race honors me with its lips, but its heart is far from me'" (Mt 15:8). We never want God to say that to us, yet we wonder if we are giving God merely lip service at times when we pray. How often, at prayer, or shortly after prayer, could we say with Hamlet: "My words fly up, my thoughts remain below: Words without thoughts never to heaven go." But that is one thing we can avoid at Mass; for, there, expressive though each word be, each is next to mute when compared to the whisperings of a heart that is right with God's great Heart, and is filled with a right intention to offer God to God on behalf of the world.

Adoration is man's prime duty and ultimate function. Adoration is the first formal purpose of Mass. Hence, the first thing that God, the "Searcher of hearts" finds in your heart at Mass is this longing of yours to adore Him as He should be adored. That is why you came to church this morning. That is why you bend your knee, fold your hands, bow your head. Your heart tells you that you are a creature and that you should adore your Creator. This internal orientation of your being finds external expression in your gestures of reverence. Rejoice in the reality that you adore your God "in Christ Jesus" who is the world's most perfect Adorer. Paul gave us God's plan when he wrote his Ephesians about the divine determination to "gather all creation both in heaven and on earth under one head, Christ" (Eph 1:10). One of the prime purposes of that "recapitulation" is adoration. Man and the universe, in its own way, is instinct with adoration. So God hears your heart at Mass singing *Adoro Te, devote* — "Devoutly, do I adore Thee." You are being true to yourself even as you are being true to your God.

But adoration is not unqualified. You are not only a creature, you are a child of God. Hence your adoration will be grateful adoration and your gratitude will be adoring thankfulness; not only for what God has made you, but for what God is! There will be a *Te Deum* in your heart even while there is a *Gloria in excelsis* on your lips; for you would pour out praise to Him who is all-holy, and who has given you a share in His all-holy nature.

Another song in your soul, whether you recognize it or not, is recognized by God who hears you singing what Mary sang when she was at Ain Karin. Your soul is singing: *Magnificat* — "My soul magnifies the Lord." How could it be otherwise since you realize that God has made you great by creation, then enhanced that greatness by re-creation when He placed you "in Christ Jesus"? Many of us want for words when we try to thank our God for all that He has done for us, to us, in us. That is why we can be grateful that He is "Searcher of our minds and hearts."

Adoration, praise, thanksgiving go up to God who is our Maker and our Father, but since we are also children of Adam and Eve our hearts must say more than *Adoro Te, Te Deum, Gloria,* and *Magnificat;* there is need for *Miserere*. Once again we can be glad that we are "in Christ Jesus," and that it is "through Jesus Christ" that we make reparation for our own sins and for those of the world. And once again we can be grateful that God is "Searcher of our hearts," for it is deep in our hearts that we all sing *Miserere*. Each of us is conscious that we were born in sin, and that we have not been sinless since birth. Hence, at Mass we are Magdalen at the feet of Christ with tears of repentance flowing; we are the Publican in the temple beating our breasts and not daring to raise our eyes to heaven; we are the Good Thief confessing God to be God, and asking a remembrance now that He is in His Kingdom. And God hears our hearts; for Love always listens.

While it is true that our hearts and whole being speak our *Miserere* from the prayers at the foot of the altar on through the stately, steady progress of the Holy Sacrifice, nowhere, perhaps, do we manage to phrase the pulsing plea for forgiveness more eloquently than at the *Nobis quoque peccatoribus* . . . where we strike our breasts in open confession of our sinfulness and plead with God for fellowship in His Kingdom with His stalwarts. . . . "To us sinners," we say, "Thy servants, who hope in the multitude of Thy mercies, grant some part, some fellowship with Thy Apostles and Martyrs. . . ." This magnificent prayer merits close study. It is pity's cry for pity; we poor beggars, who have received so much mercy, beg for more. We need it. We expect to receive it. For we beg with "hope in the multitude of God's mercies." That hope makes us bold enough to ask for some little place in that company brilliant with love, with loyalty, with fearlessness and fortitude.

We ask fellowship with John the Baptist who pointed out the Lamb who took away the sins of the world, the man who told a kinglet of his hideous sin — and paid for his courageous candor with his head. We ask to stand somewhere near Stephen, who so angered the Jews of his day by telling them of their sin that he died under a storm of stones, praying, nevertheless, that God would not "lay this latest sin to their charge." We beg to be somewhere near Matthias — and what a note the sounding of his name strikes in the soul! Matthias was the man who took the place of Judas in the apostolic band, making reparation in some way for that crime which culminated not in the kiss of betrayal, but in that deeper betrayal marked by a halter — a betrayal of trust in the mercy of God. We have been like Judas in our betrayals of God. Now we pray to be like Matthias so that we can repay.

We should know more than the mere names of these men and women with whom we beg fellowship. We should know something of the nature of their witness to Christ. For our hearts would have us witnessing in some similar fashion. We beg God to give us some share in the company of Barnabas, Paul's companion, who later parted from him in disagreement, but who never parted from Christ. We would stand near Ignatius of Antioch, that stalwart old Bishop who gave us that magnificent phrase about being "God's grain" and the "wheat of Christ." We beg God to grant us the companionship of Alexander, the Pope who ordered that water be added to the wine in every Mass. It is here in this prayer we recognize ourselves to be weak as water, yet hope in the mercy of God to make us strong as wine.

The "Searcher of hearts" hears the keen consciousness that is ours of our sinfulness accompanied by the burning desire to be strong with the strength of Christ. He hears the double beat of our hearts, one as an Act of Contrition for our sins, the other as an Act of Hope for sinlessness. That is the systole and diastole of this prayer beginning with *"Nobis quoque peccatoribus. . . ."* God hears our profound sorrow and our soaring hope as we beg for fellowship with Marcellinus and Peter, the first was a priest, the second only an exorcist; but both were strong enough with love to stand out as "the two victors" in that fiercest of all fierce persecutions — that of Diocletian. We are asking much; but we are asking "in Him and through Him" who said: "Ask; and you shall receive."

This magnificent prayer moves on and has us asking for companionship with seven women martyrs. Their sex, their youth, their various stations in life, all speak to us and for us. We tell our listening God that we would be near Perpetua and Felicity; the former a young noblewoman of twenty-two, mother of a young child who was used to tempt Perpetua to default; Felicity was a slave, mother of several children, and pregnant at time of her arrest. She delivered her child while in prison and, as the ancient chronicler put it: "came from blood to blood; from the midwife to the gladiator, to wash after her travail in a second Baptism." Perpetua, the patrician, demanded proper dress from the tribune before she would go to the amphitheater, then arranged her hair stylishly, took Felicity by the hand, and proudly went forth to martyrdom. The joyousness of such company is boon to us in these dark days.

After Perpetua and Felicity we name five young virgins with whom we would associate. Some of these were snatched from their drawing rooms and dragged to public brothels to suffer what St. Ambrose called the "double martyrdom, one of modesty, the other of religion." Agatha is supposed to have told her judge, the Roman governor, that "his words were but wind, his promises only rain, his menaces but passing floods," and assured him that no matter how hardly these things fell upon her, she would not be moved "for she was founded on rock," the Rock of Christ.

Agnes, the tender lamb of God, a mere thirteen years of age, yet wiser far than any of the ancients among the pagan Romans. It is said that "no fetters could be found small enough for her wrists." We can say that no measure can be found large enough for her heart.

Cecilia is next on our list. She brings music into our litany; for this protectress of Rome is looked upon as patroness of music. She died under Marcus Aurelius. The mention of her name should exorcise any pagan stoicism that might lurk in our minds or hearts. Marcus Aurelius' sayings have lived too long. He has been adjudged a great and a good man, but Cecilia should have us challenging that judgment.

In Lucy and Anastasia, enshrined next in the Liturgy, we find East and West united. Lucy, denounced by her betrothed, shows the West at its most valiant; while Anastasia, said to have been a pupil of Chrysogonus, named early in Mass, joins not only the Greek and Roman world, but the ends of Christ's life as well; for she died on Christ's birthday — Christmas — and her name means "Resurrection."

We would know companionship with these martyrs in our day of martyrdom in both the East and the West as the new barbarism called Communism treats Christians as did Nero, Trajan, Diocletian, and the other barbarous emperors of Rome. We weak Christians need to pray this *Nobis quoque peccatoribus* and beg *aliquam partem* — "some little part" — beg also that *societatem* — that "comradeship" with these martyrs of old. But we beg it always *non aestimator meriti* — not banking on any merits of our own, but *veniae largitor* relying on His mercies who is our Lover, our Father, our God.

You may tell me that you have never offered Mass with such knowledge of these martyrs, nor with such realization of the personal references in these prayers. But please be reminded that the priest at the altar is your representative; he is the mediator between

yourselves and your God. Then you must never forget that the
Principal Offerer of this and every Mass is Jesus Christ. Therefore,
it can be said with truth that the "Searcher of hearts" listens and
hears the Sacred Heart whenever Mass is offered.

But, pleased as God must be as He listens to every Mass, He
must be most especially pleased when He hears you, though your
representative, and "in Christ Jesus" saying: "Instructed by Thy
saving precepts, and following Thy divine instructions, we make
bold to say: *Our Father . . .*" We can make bold with the boldness
of well-loved children, for we "have received a spirit of adoption
as sons, in virtue of which we cry Abba — Father! . . . The Spirit
himself joins his testimony to that of our spirit that we are children
of God" (Rom 8:15, 16).

As you know, this prayer comes after the Canon proper has
ended. It is most fitting; for no mere man-made prayer would ever
carry on the sublime majesty found in the Canon or be compatible
with the sacredness that follows the Consecration. No prayer, save
that taught us by Christ Himself — the *Our Father* — could form
fitting transition from the Consecration to Communion. Nor could
any be found or fashioned that would suggest the unity that marks
the Church of old, the Church of today, and the Church of tomorrow. For two thousand years, children of the one Father have
lifted their minds and hearts just as we do ours in the one cry of
"Abba — Father." As long as this earth lasts and there are children
of God on it, that same cry will be heard.

This magnificent prayer expresses the heart of each of us, and
the very heart and the whole mystery of mankind. It also sums up
the entire Mass as it moves from adoration and thanksgiving to
expiation and petition: those four purposes of Calvary and every
Mass. In it are found the most majestic phrases that will ever
leave human lips as well as the most profound longings of any
and every human heart. Small wonder the Greek Liturgy of St.
James introduces this prayer with the plea: "Make us worthy, O
Lord, who lovest mankind, with freedom and without condemnation, with a clean heart, with soul enlightened, and with unashamed

faces and holy lips, to dare to call upon Thee, our Holy God and Father in Heaven, and say: *'Our Father . . .'* "

Tertullian claimed that this prayer was a summation of the entire Gospel. You will see that that is no idle claim if you but study the separate petitions. How startling is the tone of the early phrases: "Hallowed be Thy name — Thy Kingdom come — Thy Will be done." They sound more like commands than humble requests. Yet we must ever remember that Christ once told Catherine of Genoa that "it is not enough to ask; you must command."

You must see that this prayer epitomizes the Canon of Mass, as well as Mass itself; for what is Mass but a doing of His will, praying that His Kingdom come, and a hallowing of His name? It is also perfect summation of our hearts and minds; for we would know and love God as He is; we would show our love by doing His will; we would make holy His name and spread His Kingdom by our works and prayers.

But while the glory of God and the advance of His Kingdom is our primary aim, it is His will that we never forget ourselves. The beauty of life is that we are doing the will of God on earth even as it is done in heaven when we ask — and again it sounds more like a command than a petition — "Give us this day our daily bread." True, Christ once said: "It is not by bread alone that man lives . . ."; yet it is by bread *also*. God answers this petition even though there are men on earth who pretend to believe that there is no such thing as Divine Providence which sees to it that seeds die and produce a hundredfold, that mill wheels turn that wheat may be made into flour, that ovens hold heat that dough may be turned into bread. Your heartfelt *Pater noster* can offset before God this kind of thinking on the part of others; for you can expiate by your petitioning, since every bit of begging you do is true adoration because it is a confession of the sovereignty of God.

We beg for bread, earthly bread, it is true; but we are also begging for that Bread which came down from heaven, the living Bread which means eternal life for us. And when we receive this Bread God will hear in our hearts forgiveness for all those who "have trespassed against us" — and God will forgive us all our "trespasses."

But we must never forget that God "searches the heart"; hence, we must "forgive our brethren from our heart" (Mt 18:25), for all true forgiveness must come from the heart. As we say the "Our Father" we will recall Christ's own injunction about leaving our gift before the altar if we remember anyone who holds something against us, and going to settle our score with our brother, before we offer our gift — ourselves. This petition about "forgive us our trespasses as we forgive those who trespass against us" is but application of that parable Christ once told about the merciless debtor. Our Father, who is in heaven, will forgive us as we forgive others. He will take us at our word in this prayer, the *Pater Noster*. But how could anyone be without full and final forgiveness for all human trespasses when he is about to receive the Divine Guest into his soul — He who won forgiveness for all our trespasses which were infinitely more serious, since they were against our infinite God?

"Lead us not into temptation . . ." "Temptation" once had the meaning of "torture" — and it is well to pray this divinely taught prayer for those who are facing torture in so large a section of our world today. They are our brothers. Many of them fellow members of the Mystical Body.

When you realize that Mass is offered by the Mystical Body you will come to understand that God who "searches the mind and heart" actually hears the Blood of Jesus Christ as He listens to your heart and mine in every Mass. That Blood now beats in His glorified Body, but it is the Blood that was shed for our sins that we might be born again, and this time "born of God." God hears that Blood pleading as never did any blood plead since the creation of the world. Abel's was the first human blood to cry to heaven. St. Paul reminds us of that, and contrasts its cry with the one God hears as priests bend over chalices and say: "This is the chalice of My Blood, of the new and eternal Covenant, which shall be shed for you and for many for the remission of sins." Small wonder Paul says this Blood "speaks more eloquently than Abel's" (Heb 12:24). Abel's cried for vengeance. Christ's calls for mercy.

Because God hears this Blood in Mass you can take Paul's words as addressed to yourself: "Therefore, brothers, we have confident access to the Holy Place, thanks to the blood of Jesus, by following the new and living path which he has opened for us through the veil — I mean his flesh; and we have a high priest in charge of the house of God. So, let us draw near with a sincere heart, in full assurance of faith, with our hearts purified from an evil conscience, and with our bodies washed in pure water. Let us cling without faltering to the hope which we profess, for he who has given us the promise is faithful" (Heb 10:19–23).

With confidence, then, approach your God and as immediate preparation for your loving embrace of Him in Holy Communion let Him hear you saying the same prayers as does the celebrant. You will never find any better. For these plead for everything mankind needs, and for the very things your soul longs for. Make them your own.

The first of these prayers takes you back to the Cenacle; for it opens with the words: "O Lord Jesus who said to Thy Apostles, 'Peace I leave with you, My peace I give unto you,' look not upon my sins, but upon the faith of Thy Church. . . ." What wisdom in that plea! It really begs God to keep His eyes off your liabilities; to turn away from those actualities that might justly arouse His anger — those meannesses that have sprung from pride, covetousness, lust, anger, envy, gluttony, and sloth. Do not look at those things, it begs, but see me at my best; look at me in the Church, see me as Christ's mystical member, engulfed, as it were, in the faith of that Body, saturated with the holiness of that Body, sacred with the sacredness of that Body, and hear me pleading for peace: peace to the Church; peace to those who seem to hate peace; peace to all mankind. If all are enjoying peace then we can hope for that unity Christ prayed for in this same Cenacle: "that they

all may be one as we are one — I in them and you in me" (Jn
17:22). What other meaning has Mass and Communion but God's
peace, God's unity, God's love?

The second prayer is even more moving. It is a plea for pardon
and an expression of your yearning for indissoluble union with
Christ, with the Father to whom He is the Way, and with the
Spirit who is the Spirit of Love. "Never let me be separated from
Thee. . . ." Can love ask more? That is the kind of union you
ask for in this prayer of preparation. God, who loves to be asked
for those things which mean much to Him, and everything to His
creatures, listens to this prayer with a love that must be very near
to the love with which He loves Himself.

The final prayer holds the plea that this Holy Communion may
never "turn to your judgment and your condemnation." That is
complete expression of your complete distrust of yourself. It must
please God greatly to hear us profess our utter abandonment to
His goodness and love. Then you go on to plead that this personal
meeting with your God which culminates in this "wondrous exchange" wherein there is a commingling of Flesh with flesh, Blood
with blood, wherein there is a sharing of His divinity and reception
of His humanity, be for you a safeguard for soul and body in time
and a pledge of resurrection and glory with Him in eternity.

Those are very personal prayers, and it is well to realize that
though Mass is a communal act, it is also personal in the profoundest sense of the word. We lift the chalice and offer it *pro
nostra et totius mundi salute* — "for our own salvation and that
of the rest of the world." There is such a thing as a salutary selfishness. God commanded us to love ourselves. The answer we give
the priest as he turns after the Offertory and says *Orate Fratres*
— "Pray brethren" — gives the order God wants love to observe
— even in this greatest Act of Love. We reply: "May the Lord
receive the Sacrifice at thy hands to the praise and glory of His
name, to our benefit, and that of all His Church." We must love
God first; no one before Him; no one as much as Him; no one

except for and in Him. Then we must love ourselves with this proper and salutary selfishness. Finally, we must love all others.

Since that is the way God wants us to pray Mass, He will want to hear us making many personal pleas. That is the purpose of those Mementoes — one for the living, the other for the dead. You can make those as long as you desire. You can pray for all your loved ones and for every necessary gift: health, sufficient wealth, success in business, school, vocation, social world; for bread and butter; for a raise in salary; for sales this day; for sense in our teen-agers; for amicable relations with in-laws. You can pray for anything and everything in Mass, and be sure that God will listen with love. Of course He knows our needs better than we do. Nevertheless, He wants to be asked. So itemize your every desire. God will grant every one that is for your good.

When lovers meet, heart speaks to heart. Mass is a meeting of lovers. So let your heart speak to God about your relatives, friends, enemies; tell Him about your work, about your present, your past, and your future; about your successes and failures; your hopes and expectations — your every need. His Heart will listen! Do not hesitate to tell Him everything. He wants to listen — for in listening He hears not only the love of your heart but the adoration of your whole being. For every plea for help is a confession of your own impotence and His omnipotence; it is an act of humility; for it is an admission of your dependence and confession of His paternal providence. It is praise; for in telling your indigence, you are proclaiming His wealth. Your every request is a tribute of honor and glory to Him to whom all honor and glory are due.

And the beauty of it is: He will understand! Those humans who love us most and love us best do not always understand either our wishes or our words. But with God, our greatest Lover, there is never a question about His clearly understanding every wish and putting proper interpretation on every word. He listens. He hears. He loves. So let your heart speak to His Heart throughout the

Holy Sacrifice but most especially at those Mementos — one for the living, the other for the dead.

It may console you greatly to know that God actually hears your heart saying what David, that "man after His own Heart," sang, namely:

> How good is the Lord to the true of heart!
> How good is the Lord to the single-minded man! . . .

> Oh, when my mind gave way to bitter thoughts
>   and when my heart was piqued,
> I was a fool and did not understand; . . .

> But I shall always be with you;
> for you have taken hold of my right hand.

> And by your counsel you will lead me on
> and take me up to glory in the end.

> What else is there for me in heaven but you?
> And, if I am with you, the earth has no delights for me.

> My flesh is wasting, wasting in my heart:
> the firm rock of my heart, my portion, is God eternally! . . .

> For me, how good it is to be near God,
> To make the Lord, my God, my safe retreat!
>   (Ps 72:1–2, 21–22, 23–26, 28)*

That is what your heart says when you offer Mass as Pius XII exhorted you to offer: "not by the general intention . . . but by uniting yourself closely and of set purpose with the High Priest and His minister on earth."

One of the best ways of doing that, of course, is by saying and doing what the "minister on earth" is saying and doing; for that is exactly what the High Priest (Christ) is saying and doing. In other words, follow the Missal as rubrically as does the celebrant. If you happen to do that you will find yourself saying at the climax of this Act of Love: "May the Body of our Lord Jesus Christ preserve my soul unto life everlasting. May the Blood of our Lord Jesus Christ preserve my soul unto life everlasting."

But should you prefer some other manner of offering Mass than

---

* Kleist-Lynan translation.

that of using the Missal, let your heart be heard saying the same thing as the priest says when receiving the Body and Blood of our Lord; for that is precisely why God comes as Food and Drink: to preserve your soul unto life everlasting. For He is a Lover who wants to love you forever. And that is what your heart will say if you "unite yourself closely and of set purpose" as the Pope advised.

He who grants you love's second intimacy as He listens to your heart will be most anxious to grant you the third intimacy of love: that of touch. For what He hears in your heart when it is "united with the High Priest" is: *"Into Thy hands* I commend my spirit." Not that you are going to die, but because you are going to *live!*

CHAPTER EIGHT

GOD TAKES YOU IN HIS HANDS — AT MASS

Love's Third Intimacy

At the end of every Mass you say much about Christ being the Light of the world. You insist that "He enlightens every man who comes into this world." You know this Light to be the Word who "was with God and who is God," and you genuflect in adoration, appreciation, and what should be grateful love when you proclaim the fact that "the Word became flesh" (Jn 1:1–6).

That final statement tells us emphatically that it was not from outer space that the Light of the World shone upon men. He burned in our midst! He still does. The eternal God who stepped into Time at Nazareth, and was made manifest at Bethlehem, is still with us. As He was then, so is He now: the Light of the World burning among men to enlighten all men. Transubstantiated Bread and Wine is the Flesh and Blood of that burning Light; it is the humanity as well as the divinity of Jesus Christ; and He is there for the same purpose He had when He came among us originally: "that we might become the holiness of God." But that purpose will never be attained unless there is an embrace of love; an embrace that will unite and transform; a union that will give us, within our very bodies and souls, the life of God. That purpose will be attained only if God takes us to Himself "in Christ Jesus" and "through Jesus Christ" in Mass and Holy Communion.

As Omnipotence, Omniscience, Infinite Holiness, God was so distant that personal contact with Him was our despair. St. Paul tells us as much again and again. But this omnipotent, omniscient,

126

all-holy God entered human life. He became a baby, grew to be a man, and finally became a corpse. Why? — That just as that Corpse came to know a Resurrection and Glorification, so we men might come to know and love to such a degree that we might be changed into His very holiness.

That is commonplace among instructed Catholics. But because it is commonplace it loses nothing of its truth, its transcendence, its almost terrifying intimacy — terrifying and intimate because implicit in this commonplace is God's personal demand for a personal response from us men.

You live in a world that is in ferment. The very ground is shaking under your feet. You look around in fright, and grope for something stable. You are one palpitating plea for security. And your whole being is alive with longing for truth that is tangible and unchangeable. You have them all in Him who is Mass. Christ Jesus said of Himself: "I am the Way, the Truth, the Life." He is all three because what St. John said of Him is basic, essential: He is Love.

Many of your present-day, sophisticated writers like to insist that your world is extremely complex, and your fellowmen pronouncedly confused. But is not all such talk noise and nonsense? Is it not forgetting that God, who is the Simplest of all simple beings, came into our midst to unravel all complexity and resolve all confusion?

Of course the intelligentsia want nothing to do with anything that is offered as a simplification. In their smug smartness they condemn it out of hand as an "oversimplification" and imply that he who offers it is not only simple but something of a simpleton. They have a similar "complex" (oh, yes! these bright people have "complexes" — many more and much more complex than the ordinary intelligent person ever has) against any of the traditional solutions or familiar answers. With what looks like a very real "compulsion" they seek always the new, the unfamiliar, the untried. They insist that we are in a "new world," are walking on a "new earth," amid "new people." One wonders if they will soon demand a new savior for this new world; a new light for this new darkness. Then one wonders even more if they realize that they are actually in the dark.

Jesus said: "I am the light of the world. He who follows me will not walk in the dark, but have the light of life" (Jn 8:12). The Evangelist tells us these words were spoken "in the treasury while speaking in the temple." Then Christ repeated this teaching the first Palm Sunday of the world but with a more insistent ring to His words. Just after predicting the way He would be Victim on His First Mass He said: "A little while longer will the light be among you. Walk while you have the light, or darkness will overtake you. He who walks in the dark does not know where he is going. As long as you have the light, believe in the light so that you may become sons of light" (Jn 12:35).

That is simple enough, utterly uncomplicated, and free from all confusion. It sublimates to: "Follow Me." And that was, is, and ever will be the one answer given by God's only Son to all questions by men. It applies today as well as it did two thousand years ago. It will apply two thousand years from now. The quintessence of that following of Christ is Mass. That is why we have tried to resolve all complexities, and do away with all possible confusion by giving you the living God in His greatest Act of Love — one which He commanded us to "do." We have presented it as the simplest and most satisfying way to relate religion to life; or, better, as the one way to live.

It is fashionable today — at least in print — to point the finger at almost everyone alive and accuse them of being "numb souls," "inert," "hopeless," or "despairing." It is also fashionable to turn on those who give the very answers of God to modern man's questionings, and decry them for "verbalizing on suffering and submission" for "giving a few pious phrases about the Cross and Salvation," but never seeking modern man "in his spiritual wilderness with all its baffling problems." One cannot pardon these men as ignorant and pass off their tirades as lack of information. They speak of the Cross. They must know something of Jesus Christ.

How is it, then, that they miss the very heart of His message, the purpose of His mission, the simplicity and clarity of His statement "Do this . . ."? Have they heard that command? Have they realized it simply means: Make Mass your life, and your life Mass?

When you hear such intellectuals crying imperiously for something "new," quietly remind them of the opening of St. Paul's Epistle to the Hebrews: "In many fragmentary and various utterances, God spoke to our ancestors through the prophets; at the present time, the final epoch, *he has spoken to us through his Son . . .*" (Heb 1:1, 2).

God is still speaking to us "through His Son"; for God's plan for us men is simplicity itself. He would save us. Therefore, He sent His Son to be "the Way, the Truth, and the Life." That Son showed us the way, gave us the truth, won for us the life — in and through His Mass. But that is not all; nor is that the end. He would not leave us orphans. He would remain in our midst to show us the way, give us the truth, share with us the life. He would do it through His Church — His Mystical Body. Through and in that Body He will save us whom He has already redeemed. He will do so through His Sacraments and His Sacrifice through which He will so unite us to Himself as to transform us and make us not only presentable to the Father, but acceptable by that Father.

What is complicated or confusing about that? The will of the Father and the will of the Son are one; for they are in love. That one will is our salvation. To effect that salvation the Father sent the Son; the Son established His Mystical Body; and in that Mystical Body we are His members. Therefore, we must do as Christ did. We must do as Christ now does! We must do the will of the Father. We must save men. But there is only one way to do that — His way! He offered Mass. He told us to do the same.

It is relatively easy to see how to make Christ's Mass our life; for the slightest bit of theological thinking will convince us that since Mass is Christ Himself, risen from the dead, given to us under sacramental signs to be the Sacrifice we offer to God, it follows that herein, implicitly if not explicitly, is all we believe; herein lies the Power that sustains us, the Food that nourishes us, the Act that answers the deepest need and cry of our being to be united to God. But how is Mass to become the very life we lead, or, in other words, how is our life to become Mass?

That question has been posed by some of the best instructed Catholics. They frown and ask: "What is required — just my intention to offer everything 'in Christ Jesus'?" That, certainly. But more than that. Everything — and that is to be taken literally — everything is to be offered *as Jesus Christ.*

The only Son of God redeemed us *principally* through His Passion, Death, Resurrection, and Ascension. That italicized word — *principally* — is taken from the teachings of the Council of Trent. Implicitly that word tells you and me that Christ redeemed by other actions than those of Holy Week and the Easter Season. The point here is that Christ did not become a Priest only in the Cenacle any more than He became Victim only on the Cross. Christ was Priest from His conception. His every work, then, was the work of a priest, though not necessarily a "liturgical" offering. In other words He was redeeming us during His Flight into Egypt and while dwelling in Nazareth just as well as when He was stumbling on His way to Calvary or speaking those Seven Last Words from the Cross. His every act was an act of a Person who was divine, who was using His assumed human nature as His conjoined instrument in the one work His Father had given Him to do: the redemption of mankind. Hence, every action of the Man-God was of infinite worth and infinitely pleasing to the Father. His slightest sigh in that human body of His was enough to redeem ten thousand worlds ten thousand times more sinful than ours. But His Father willed a holocaust. Christ fulfilled that will; for Christ loved the Father.

The point of the parallel is this: you are His member not only when you offer the Holy Sacrifice of Mass but so long as you live in that body of flesh and blood which is yours. Therefore, you are a priest of the great high God not only when in Church for liturgical worship, but every hour of the day and every hour of the night, no matter where you spend those hours. Hence, it is possible for you to make every act an act of a priest — by intention, of course, but also by attention to your role in this world: God's will for you as an individual.

The doctor should ever be mindful that he is the "extension" of the Divine Physician, the Only Priest of the New Law. Hence, while functioning as medical man or surgeon, he is also functioning as priest; for the character of priesthood is much more deeply and indelibly on his soul than any professional air he may have acquired. Then he can realize that Carlyle was right when he said something to the effect that "whoever touches the human body lays hand on God." That will increase the aura of sacredness there should ever be about his work. But deeper than any of this will be his awareness that he has one ultimate work to do as he functions as a physician, and that is to offer Mass. Hence, he can make of every somatic or psychic complaint the water, the wheat, and the wine he needs for his oblation. The intention to be and do all this can be made at his Morning Offering, but the attention should be ever present, at least on the fringe of his consciousness, and can be renewed from time to time throughout his day. It is "Christ-consciousness" that is required: the consciousness that he "lives and moves and has his being" *in Christ Jesus,* and that he has been made a priest that he might aid the Only Priest in the application of the merits won by His Redeeming Act of Calvary.

The lawyer and the teacher will be mindful of the fact that Christ, the Priest, was the Teacher of the New Law, and the New Law's real Lawgiver. Hence, His every act as Lawyer and Teacher was the act of a Priest. They will, then, make all their acts the same; for they are His members with His one work to continue.

The same is true of every other profession and every other occupation. Awareness of who we are, and of what we have been empowered to do, will have us taking every tiniest detail of our everyday lives and seeing them as so much matter for our offertory. Whatever be our "state in life" it is filled to the full with "wheat, water, and wine" that can be offered "in Christ Jesus" and *as Jesus Christ* to God so that He can "bless, approve, ratify, make worthy and acceptable" for "transubstantiation."

The love of husband and wife; the care parents lavish on children; the discharge of duty in office, shop, store, or on the street, is to be offered to God. And God will accept them if Christ says over them: "This is My Body"; and He will say that if we make offering as priests!

The phrase "in Christ Jesus" takes on ever deeper meaning, does it not, as we probe more deeply into life and proper living? It permeates not only our whole personal being, but fills everything we do with the holiness of God, when we live and function conscious of who we are and what we are on earth to do.

This whole matter of making our lives Mass can be simplified (with anything but an "oversimplification") by the one word *obedience*.

Jesus Christ did not redeem mankind by suffering. Jesus Christ did not repair the shattered fabric of creation by dying. Jesus Christ did not reconcile sinful man with the all-holy God by thorns, scourge, nails, or lance. Jesus Christ re-created the universe by *obedience;* or, better still by love — for what is obedience in root, stem, and flower but love for the one commanding? "The Father loves me," said Christ, "because I lay down my life, and he wills that I should take it back again. No one can rob me of it. No, I lay it down of my own will. I have the power to lay it down, and power to take it back again. *Such is the charge I have received from my Father"* (Jn 10:18 ff.).

Love, then, expressed in obedience, is fullest explanation of Christ's Mass — and of yours. You obey God best when you perform every duty of your state in life simply because it *is* God's will for you. So the mother at the washing machine or at the ironing board; the wife at the sink over the dishes or at the stove over the meat for the table; the husband and father at his desk, bench, or wherever he works; the single person tidying his or her room: all are obeying God; for each is performing some duty of his or her state in life. Each, then, has all that is required to make their lives Mass — and thus bring themselves to holiness. For as Lacordaire said: "Duty done spells sanctity." Who could doubt it when he realizes that obedience is love; love a union of wills; and sanctity a share in the life of God which Christ won for us by so loving the Father as to do His Will? Hence, love is shown best by "doing always the things that please Him" — the duties of one's state in life.

This simplification not only clarifies Christ's Mass for you, but shows you your position in life most clearly: you are *mediator Dei et hominum* (1 Tim 2:5) — a priest, a mediator between God and men — at every hour of the day and night so long as you live on earth. "Every priest is chosen from among men and appointed to serve men in what concerns the worship of God. He is to offer gifts and sacrifices in expiation of sins" (Heb 5:1). That is St. Paul's description of the high-priestly office. It can be, and should be, applied by you to your office as participator in the priesthood of Christ. The "gifts and sacrifices" you are to offer are the duties of your state in life. Once you come to understand just what the word "sacrifice" means, you will come to see that anything and everything that comprises your life and its duties is matter for Sacrifice.

Too few of our contemporaries understand this word in its root meaning; hence, they shy from what they should embrace, and run away from what should be the real substance of their lives, and the truest joy in all their living. That is true even of some educated Catholics. They associate privation, suffering, pain with the word. But such an association of ideas is to hear notes but never catch the melody; to listen to words but never catch the meaning of sentences; to look at parts but never see the whole. There is some partial truth in this association of ideas; but it is that partial association which makes of the truth something close kin to a lie.

Sacrifice is the act of a lover who cannot find words for his love. Wisely he resorts to signs and symbols. He takes things, offers them to his beloved, and has them speak with eloquence what his lips cannot say, but what his heart would have his beloved hear. Gifts are the language of love; and the one message they convey is: "I love you." When courting a woman a man will "say it with flowers," with music, with candy, with books. He will "say it" with many gifts; and, ultimately, each will say: "I love you so much that I would give you my very self."

But there is a deeper depth yet to go before we are at the root of this meaningful word. Sacrifice derives from two Latin words: *sacrum,* meaning "sacred," and *facere,* which means "to make." Hence, when we make a sacrifice we *make a thing sacred.* But how can we sinful humans make anything sacred? In one way only: by giving it to God, who alone is sacred. Consequently, in its most radical meaning, sacrifice is simply a *gift-giving to God.* Since gifts are signs of love, sacrifice is making love to God.

This is the most personal and, in a way, the profoundest aspect of your function as a priest. You are a lover who would speak to God in accents that are laden with love, and be united with God and with all He loves! Hence you will offer gifts to God every hour of the day and every hour of the night; and each will say what every love gift is meant to say: "I love you so entirely that I would give you my very self."

I have just come from acting as a priest liturgically. I have just offered Mass. But, as I sit here typing, I am still a priest; and this act of typing is the act of a priest, though, in a liturgical sense, it is not a priestly act. It is not offering Christ's Mass, but it is offering my Mass; for I am ever conscious that I am His member, which means that I am ever and always a priest. Since I know well that the particular function of a priest is to offer Mass, which means to make love, I try to make my every act an act of love and part of my Mass.

Soon I shall go out dressed not in vestments for His Mass, but in what I look upon as "vestments" for my Mass. I will go out in my work clothes. I will weed an onion patch, pick strawberries, cultivate cabbages, tie up tomatoes. Those, of course, are the acts of a farmer. But this farmer is a priest of God; so his farming

will be the actions of a priest. Since I do all things "in Christ
Jesus" and *as Jesus Christ,* each of those acts will be the act of
a lover, offering these lowly deeds as symbols and signs of my
love for God and His people.

If that be not true, what a waste of time I am guilty of, and
what a prostitution of my priestly powers! But it is true — true
with the very truth of God; for St. Paul was under God's own
inspiration when he wrote: "Whether you eat or drink, or do anything else, do everything for God's glory . . . try to conciliate all
men seeking not your own advantage but that of the many in order
to save them" (1 Cor 10:31–33). And again: "Glorify the God
in your body" (1 Cor 6:20).

You see, then, how simple and sacred this makes all life and
all living. I am obeying God; but obedience is love in action;
therefore I am loving as I labor. My hands may be performing
the acts of a laborer, but my heart is the heart of a priest, and the
works of my hands are but symbols and signs of the ceaseless song
of my priestly heart. My labor is not the Liturgy of His Mass,
but it is "liturgical" — since it is my Mass. Further, my every
breath and heartbeat is referred to Him who is in the Host and
the consecrated Wine. Everything I do is done "in union with the
Holy Sacrifice of the Mass" which is being offered somewhere in
the world every split second of time. So Mass is my life, and my
life is Mass.

What is true of me and my day should be true of you and your
day. You offer His Mass to make you more fit to offer your Mass.
For every person who leaves church after meeting God in His
Act of Love called Mass goes forth to work or to his home as a
person purified. It is Christ Himself who said: "Now you are clean
by reason of the word I have spoken to you" (Jn 15:3). You
have heard Him speaking directly and personally to you in His
Mass. You have seen Him. You have touched Him. You have
taken Him into your body. You go forth, then, radiating Christ.
Anyone who sees, hears, or touches you, should be sanctified by
the contact by reason of the Holy One within you; and everything

you look upon, touch, or take up should be so much matter for your offertory in your Mass, which you offer "in Christ Jesus" — and *as Jesus Christ*.

This, of course, is not automatic. Physical presence will not bring you these results from Mass. You must have been present as a person and participated as a priest. You must have opened yourself to the Light of the World and allowed Him to pour Himself into your darkness, so that you can be transformed into a "child of light" and be made "lightsome" — filled with that Light which is Love.

Love — that is the operative word; for one does not begin to live until one has begun to love. Then it is that he finds himself breaking out of the cramped, confined, and confining world that was himself. He is a discoverer who has come upon a whole new universe; and he goes on exploring a land unknown, but most alluring. When one comes to love God he will have discovered a universe that will never be fully known, but one that will be eternally alluring. To such a one you could say: "Be brave. Be bold. Be utterly unselfish. Give, and never count the cost. Seek ever new ways to give newer gifts. But be honest enough to have every gift a symbol of that total gift of self you want to give."

Since true love ever desires the presence of the beloved, wants to hear his voice, to feed on the vision of him, seeking ever to know ever more and more about him, and so craves to be like him that it will begin to imitate the beloved's ways, you can see how invitable it is for a lover of God to make his or her life a priestly life by making it a Mass. For love, when true, is a state rather than an act; it is constant and continuous. So the alert and loving Catholic goes from Christ's Mass, which is his very life, out into the world of his everyday living to make that world more Christ-filled, and that living a veritable Holy Sacrifice.

We are back to that word which means "make sacred" — which means "give-to-God." Look at the first sacrifice we know of: Abel offered a lamb to God. First he slew it; then he placed it on an altar to be burned. He was talking in love's language. He was using sign and symbol to express his heart. The essential point in this, as in every other sacrifice, is that an outward sign is used to signify inward love; a visible gift is given as symbol of that invisible self who is so in love that he craves union with the beloved.

Translate Abel's action into our own idiom. He took a lamb, for he was a herdsman, and had it stand as symbol for himself. To show God he was offering his total being, Abel slew that lamb, took its life, then burned that lifeless lamb until it was totally consumed. He was having that lamb say: "My God, I adore You as Author of my life. I am grateful for all You have given me. I would manifest my grateful and adoring love for You by offering You my whole being and all the life there is in me. But, since I cannot take my own life, let this lamb speak for me and say: 'I would give my life's blood to You. I would be one with You. That is how I love You.' If You accept this lamb as symbol of me and my life, I will know that my heart is right with Your Heart; that we are at one."

"At–one–ment." That is the derivation of our word "atonement" — and this being "at one" gives you clear insight into one of the main purposes of Christ's Sacrifice — and of all your own "in Christ Jesus" — you would be "at one" with God!

What Abel did has been done by all peoples from his time to our own. Individuals, families, tribes, whole peoples have placed something dear to them on an altar; slew, or had slain, this object of offering; then burned it as sign that it no longer belonged to them, but had been put aside as belonging to God. It had been "made sacred"; it had been "sacrificed." Frequently at the end of the ceremony there would be a meal of some sort; usually on the part of the victim offered. This proved, somehow or other, that the gift had been accepted by God and that the people were "at one" with their God. Not only that, this meal showed that they were sharing in the life of their divinity.

You see the similarity in Christ's Sacrifice to all this. There was the offering of the Victim in the Cenacle. There was the slaying of the Victim on Calvary. There was the acceptance of the Victim at the Resurrection, Ascension, and Enthronement.*

Nor can anyone miss the re-presentation of all this in Mass. True, there is no slaying of the Victim. Christ does not suffer in Mass. Christ does not die in Mass. Yet Mass is a perfect Sacrifice since the same Priest is at our altars who was in the Cenacle; the same Victim is on our altars as was on the Cross; but He is in the state in which He left the Tomb and ascended to the right hand of the Father. By virtue of that one offering, made two thousand years ago, He offers Himself in every Mass I offer, and in every Mass every other ordained priest shall offer. And He is accepted by the Father. As for the meal, the "at-one-ment" with God, and the sharing in the life of God — what is Holy Communion?

The Council of Trent put all that in a sentence saying: "It is one and the same Victim; the same Person who offers it by the ministry of His priests, who then offered Himself on the Cross, the manner of offering alone being different."

Look again at that "manner of offering being different." On Calvary He acted alone, in His own Person directly. In Mass He acts through the persons who offer and through the one who consecrates. He acts in Person, of course, but only invisibly and indirectly. He acts through me. He acts through you. Thus you cannot be a mere spectator at Mass. You cannot simply watch the Mass being offered. You must act. You must offer God to God — and be offered by God to God "in Christ Jesus."

That last point is the crucial point: you are offered to God even as you offer God to God. For Mass is that "wondrous exchange." God places Himself in your hands so that you may have fit Offering for God. But you also place yourself in God's hands to be offered by God to God. That is Mass. That is what it means to be "in Christ Jesus."

What warrant is there for making such a statement? Listen to

---

* See footnote, p. 46.

St. Augustine as he points to the bread on the paten and to the wine in the chalice: "It is *you* who lie here on the altar table; it is *you* who are in this chalice; and we ourselves are there with you." Why are you there? For the same purpose Christ is there: to be offered to God as a love-gift; to be made a sacred thing — a *theotyte*.

We have used that last word more than once about Jesus Christ as He now lives at the right hand of the Father. Perhaps we should have explained that it is a transliteration from the Greek word, which means not only placing a thing before God, but having Him accept it as a gift. He takes it to Himself as His own. That is Sacrifice. That is Mass. That is Christ today — and you, as you should be. In Mass you are offered to God, and taken by God — you are made a *theotyte*.

St. Augustine who told you that you were in the bread and wine also said: "By the Sacrifice of her Head, the Church learns to sacrifice herself." That means that from Christ she learns how to "make herself sacred" — how to become *theotyte*. For the Church who offers Christ, also offers herself "through Him, with Him, and in Him." The physical Body of Christ, in its present state of existence, that is, the glorified God-Man, constitutes, above all else, that which is offered in Mass. But, as this same Augustine so often insisted, every external sacrifice is but sign and symbol of an interior sacrifice. Therefore, in offering externally the glorified Body of Christ, the Church, which is His Mystical Body, offers Him as pledge and testimony of her own interior offering.

So there is warrant enough for all that has been said; so powerful and pointed a warrant that we would be wise never to forget what this same St. Augustine once said to his people at Carthage: "God wants *you* rather than your gifts" (Serm. 82). Further, it would be prudence on our part always to hold in mind what St. Gregory the Great once wrote: "We must offer ourselves; for Mass will be Sacrifice *for us* when we have made an offering *of us*." Pius XI put all that even more strongly in his *Miserentissimus Redemptor* when he first said: "In the very august Sacrifice the priest and the rest of the faithful must join their immolation in such a way that they offer themselves as living hosts," then concluded by asserting: "The Sacrifice of our Saviour is not celebrated with the requisite sanctity if our offering of self and the sacrifice of self correspond not to His Passion."

Obviously then, it is imperative that we realize that once we have placed ourselves on the paten and in the chalice we belong to God — not only for the few passing moments required to celebrate Mass in the morning, but during every single moment of the ensuing day. We place our whole selves into Christ's Sacrifice. Consequently, everything we do, everything we are, everything we may yet become, should be offered "in Christ Jesus" and as Jesus Christ.

This is a necessary consequence of our Baptism. For through that Sacrament we were made priests of the New Law. But in the New Law the Only Priest is also the Only Victim. Therefore, we who participate in Christ's priesthood, participate also in His victimhood.

There is another word that some modern sophisticates say that modern man does not like. I have been told by such intellectuals that men of the mid-twentieth century shy from such words as "sacrifice" and "victim." Once again I question their powers of observation. Once again I dare to say that both they and too many educated Catholics are not seeing things in focus; are not in touch with reality; that they are failing to see the whole picture.

What America has shown the world from Pearl Harbor to Nagasaki tells me that, far from shying from sacrifice and victimhood, men and women of the mid-twentieth century embraced both. They made sacrifices, and, in a sense, each became a victim — a willing victim — for each was in love with his country and all she stands for.

What has been witnessed within the cloisters of America since World War II also gives the lie to those who will look yet fail to see how noble is our baptized human nature. Gethsemani became so overcrowded shortly after the war that Trappists were actually living in tents. What happened here in Kentucky soon took place in Massachusetts, and is now going on in Iowa, Utah, Georgia, California, and New York. In place of the three thinly populated monasteries for men — and none for women — we now have twelve for men, two for women, with a third soon to come into being. These young Americans wanted to live. By some grace of God they realized that to live means to love, to love means to give, to love totally means to give total self. They would give themselves to God for His glory and the salvation of men. They would make themselves not only victims but holocausts.

Since so many of the smart moderns pose as existentialists, meet them on their own grounds and refute them with existential facts. Human nature loves to love; therefore, human nature loves to sacrifice; for sacrifice is love's most eloquent language. Clear-sighted human nature sees that the best way, the surest, safest, quickest way is *victimhood*. For us Catholics that means Mass.

But let us understand in what victimhood consists.

One who has looked at Jesus Christ with seeing eyes can grow impatient with those well-meaning, but not so well-understanding people who seem to think that the Christ-life — for Him in His physical Body, as well as for us in His mystical Body — was, and is to be, nothing but sadness, suffering, and excruciating sorrow.

One has but to look into the eyes of a newborn baby, listen to baby laughter, or feel a baby's tiny hands twine around one's finger to come in contact with some of the very glory of God. Christ was once a newborn Baby. Even then He was Priest and Victim; even then He was offering infinitely acceptable Sacrifice to God; even then He was adoring, thanking, expiating, and petitioning for mankind.

There was joy — the fruit of love — in Bethlehem's cave. There was joy also in heaven. So much so that angels ruptured the silence of the night with their *Gloria in excelsis* — the same song we sing in Mass. It was most fitting; for the Perfect Priest and the Perfect Victim was there in that cave — and part of His Mass was being offered. Yet in what *joy!*

What was true of Bethlehem was also true of Nazareth. Christ was Priest and Victim throughout His boyhood years just as really as He was when in the Cenacle He held bread in His hands, or when on the Cross those same hands were held by nails. But you can be sure that Nazareth was radiant with happiness and joy. How could it be otherwise when the King of Heaven was there as a growing boy? In that joy and happiness the same four ends of Mass mentioned above: adoration, thanksgiving, reparation, and petition, were being attained. Sacrifice — gift-giving to God — can be offered amid human joys and can actually consist in the joys God gives us humans. To be a victim like Christ, then, does not necessarily mean thorns, nails, and a lance-opened side. It means that we are to be humble enough to accept all the joy God gives us, and honest enough to offer it back to Him "in Christ Jesus"; humble enough to accept our "state in life" with joy, and honest enough to be obedient in that "state of life" and offer all our obedience to the Father, who has placed us in our particular "state of life," "in Christ Jesus" and as Jesus Christ.

Chesterton once said that "joy is the secret of Christians." Why do we keep that secret to ourselves? Or should we be asking: Have modern Christians got the secret? They seem so prone to measure only the rainfall in their lives. There is ever so much more tranquillity and splendor in the ordinary Christian's life than there are storms; and that simply because their lives are ordinarily Christian. Christ, you see, had three hours on the Cross; only three. Yet, He lived on earth thirty-three years. And again we insist He was Priest and Victim every hour of each of those years.

But do not miss the point. It is not that Jesus did not suffer. Nor is it that priesthood and victimhood, which are ours, and which require that we offer sacrifice, cannot cause pain. They can. They will. But the point here is that we are too prone to be superficial about our Christian living, and count our "crosses," while seldom totaling up our blessings. Further, we seem to forget at times that every blessing is given in the form of a cross, and that every real "cross" is a true blessing.

Every Christian will suffer. No Christian will ever suffer as much as Christ. Yet, every Christian, in his suffering, should be as joy-filled as was the Christ all the days of His earthly life, and never more so than when in the middle of His Mass and ours. Were we to look for the moment of supremest joy in Christ's earthly life, I believe we would find it to have been that moment when He cried: "It is completed." The ending of our Mass should be the same for you and for me.

Joy in sacrifice? Joy in victimhood? Joy for Christ on Calvary? Joy for us Christians as we make our lives veritable Masses? Most certainly! Nowhere with greater surety. Do not take my word for it. But do take God's word. Through St. Paul, in that Epistle which we have seen is the Epistle *par excellence* on priesthood, victim-hood, and Mass, God says: "Let us eagerly throw ourselves into the struggle before us, and persevere, with our eyes fixed on Jesus, the pioneer and perfect embodiment of confidence. He, *in view of the joy offered him,* underwent crucifixion with contempt for its disgrace, and has taken his seat at the right hand of God's throne. Meditate on him who in his person endured such great opposition at the hands of sinners; then your souls will not be overwhelmed with discouragement" (Heb 12:2, 3).

Through St. Paul, God is telling us not to run away from suffer-ing of any sort. In fact, He tells us to "throw ourselves upon it eagerly." But note well that it is stipulated that we do this only if we have our eyes fixed steadily on Christ, and see the joy He had before Him as He moved on in His Mass; joy as He stumbled and fell on the way to Calvary; joy as soldiers drove nails through hands and feet; joy as He heard the jeers of the high priests, Scribes, and Pharisees. He knew some joy even at the moment of dereliction when He cried out: "My God, my God, why do you abandon me?" (Mt 27:46) — and the greatest joy as He drew His last breath. For He was in love with God the Father — and the fruit of love is joy. Calvary with all its agony was His Father's will. Love is a union of wills. So Christ knew joy always.

Hence, if we will be true Christians, there will be nothing but joy in our hearts as we move along in the "canon" of our Mass; for our eyes will be fixed on Him who is our Joy. Life is simple. Life is sublime. For it means creaturehood for us; and creaturehood for us means Christhood; and Christhood means priesthood and victimhood. But priesthood and victimhood spell love — and the fruit of love for time and for eternity is joy.

Now you know what you ought to be doing at Mass, and what you should be getting out of Mass. In every Mass you offer Christ to God, and "in Christ Jesus" you offer yourself. You equivalently say what Christ said on Calvary: "Into Thy hands . . ." God takes you at your word. He takes you into His hands; ultimately, it is for the same purpose He received His only Son — *to glorify you!* Every Mass is for glory — God's and your own. Every Mass is that "wondrous exchange" — and from each Mass you should come forth more like unto God — "in Christ Jesus."

That is what you should be getting out of Mass: more Christ-life — for more Christ-like living. Not necessarily any feeling of being more holy; no emotional thrill — but *LIFE*.

That you will get if you make Mass what it is: an Act of Love, an "exchange" between lovers. Then you will be able to say with St. Paul: "It is now no longer I who live, but Christ lives in me. The life that I now live in this body, I live by faith in the Son of God, who loved me and sacrificed himself for me" (Gal 2:20).

EPILOGUE

"LORD, THAT THEY MAY SEE AND HEAR AND TOUCH!"

"Through him, therefore, let us continually offer to God a sacrifice" (Heb. 13:15).

Dear God, it is done. I thank You for allowing me to answer that too frequently asked question: "Why don't I get more out of Mass?" and to show those others who questioned me how to become more holy through Mass, by showing both that Mass is an Act of Love in which we tiny humans, of a very transitory life on earth, are allowed to see, to hear, to touch, and even to taste Your only Son and learn that He *"is* sweet."

Those are love's intimacies, God, as we know love. We want to see, then to hear, and finally we long to touch and become one with the beloved. In Mass these three intimacies are granted us. And wonder beyond all wonders: You reciprocate. You see us. You listen to and actually hear us. You touch us and even take us into Your hands — to transform us more and more into Yourself.

I thank You, God, for this experience. From now on every Mass, not only those You allow me to celebrate as a consecrating priest, but those also in which I am only an offering priest, will mean more to me because of this labor of love. My life will be even more Mass-conscious after this; for a more vivid realization of all that it means to be "in Christ Jesus" has come to me as I pondered over the truths I should tell my readers. I glory more and more in my priesthood and my victimhood "in Christ Jesus" and my functioning as both *as Jesus Christ.* Life will be even more joy-filled from now on; for You have shown me throughout these days of compostion that *this is love.*

145

You know, dear God, that this work has been part of my Mass. I have offered it all "through Him, with Him, and in Him" who is Your only Son; and it was offered that by it you may be loved the more. Accept it, God, for those four ends which are the purposes of every Mass. Adoration first. Yes, God, that is the prime purpose, the principal duty, the most important function of my life — as it is of every human being's. I came to Gethsemani many years back — *to adore!* But not only to adore — to repair also. So now I beg You to forgive me every defect in this effort. Pardon my impulsiveness that manifested itself now and then; my impatience — especially, dear God, with those of our day who appear so negative, yet so superior. They may be likened to some exceptionally capable physician who would diagnose faultlessly, then fail to prescribe — though the "specific" for the disease he had diagnosed was in his very hand. I realize, as well as these men, that our times are difficult. I agree that many moderns feel a deep-seated, though not always recognized, sense of guilt. But what stirs my impatience with these men is that they themselves either do not realize, or, realizing, suppress the fact, that this sense of guilt comes from living in error; from not being true to one's self; from having enthroned falsity as a veritable god. There are millions who have no order in which to live, no standard by which to judge, no Absolute in whom they can believe. Small wonder they feel guilty.

I see a Europe, dear God, that has come to hate the very image of man, and is nauseated with existence itself, because of the countless horrors visited upon the people by the megalomania of a few men in modern times.

I see an America that is angry. The old agrarian republic is gone. In its place we have a technological powerhouse. Many in our society, especially the young, are angry enough not only to challenge our culture, but even to rebel against it. They are disgusted with the materialism, the hedonism, and the paganism of so many in present-day American society. They have become angry with the rampant superficiality everywhere.

There is nothing really new in what I see here and across the ocean. I know that, dear God. It is simply man puzzled by his own existence. By a drive You planted in his very being he demands that there be meaning to life; that he have some destiny to achieve; that there be purpose for all his efforts. Many a modern, here and abroad, feels that he is without dignity simply because he cannot see his destiny. Their world is an empty world. Who wants to live, in a world that is empty, a life that has no meaning? That is the question which has always faced those who know not You!

That is why I grew impatient with those intellectuals who should see that the world, which they call "new," needs no new Savior, but desperately needs to come to Him whom You sent, God, to be their Light, their Life, their Love. If that was not holy impatience, forgive me, God, and in Your goodness see that it will effect some good.

Of course I offer this entire effort as gratitude, God; for that is the outstanding quality I want my love to ever hold. It was only today, as I completed this work, that I realized that its theme and its truth have all been summed up beautifully in what is called the "Hymn of the Society of Jesus." That "hymn" is actually the recast of a prayer St. Ignatius of Loyola, the founder of the Jesuits, often suggests in his Spiritual Exercises as a fitting conclusion to an ardent colloquy. It runs:

> Take and receive, O Lord, my liberty;
> Take all my will, my mind, my memory.
> All things I own, and all I have are Thine.
> Thine was the gift — to Thee I all resign.

That makes the offertory of our Mass. We place ourselves: all that we have and all that we are on the paten and in the chalice — and beg You to take. For we would become *theotytes*. Then, in the Society's hymn comes lines that tell clearly of that *admirabile commercium* with which I opened this book; that "wondrous exchange" which describes so fully the reality of Mass. For the sons of St. Ignatius pray:

Only Thy grace and love on me bestow;
Possessing these, all riches I forego.

That is Mass, God — both that of Your only Son, and that of us Your adopted sons. That is what life is meant to be. For that is love!

Dear God, I beg You to allow all who read this book to come to the realization that Mass is not something but Someone; that it is Your only Son in whom they live and move and have their being, "through whom, with whom, and in whom" they were born and are kept breathing to give You "all honor and glory." Let them realize that Mass, as a liturgical celebration, is an action that has beginning and end, but that Mass, as a life action, goes on after the liturgical celebration is over; and that it is in this life action that they show precisely what they got out of the liturgical action.

Dear God I want them all to be happy, to be joy-filled, in time as well as for eternity. So won't You let them know that they are members of Your only Son's Mystical Body? Hence, they can offer Mass "in Him" daily, hourly, every single moment. If they realize that, God, life can hold no real problem for them; no hour of the day or the night can be empty; nor any split second of time, sterile. For no matter what You allow to come their way, they will recognize it as something to be offered as wheat, water, and wine; something to be "transubstantiated."

How simple that will make all living for them, God. How readily they will learn how to become more and more holy. For once they take everything in life as "matter" for their Mass, they really have acquired the "mind of Christ" to which St. Paul exhorted all to aspire; for they will see everything as Your will. Then they will live in obedience; or better still, in love; for obedience is love in action. Once they acquire that orientation, God, they will have the very courage of Christ to do Your will and share in His very power to accomplish it; for they will truly live "in Christ Jesus." Thus life will have become for them what I know You planned it to be for all of us humans: a divine romance — a love affair between You and ourselves.

What complaint can anyone harbor in his mind or heart, God, no matter what disappointments, contradictions, failures, frustrations, and even defeats come their way, once they acquire the habit of offering themselves as victims "in Christ Jesus" every morning of their lives? Suffering will be felt. But it will never sadden, far less sour them; for they will know that they have offered themselves as victims in this morning's Mass, and that they will need wheat and wine and water for tomorrow's Mass.

The beauty of it all is, dear God, that they will come to recognize the fact that whatever eventuates in their lives comes to them from Your hands — and that You will never hand them anything that is not for Your glory and their own good. Such realization will have them doing what Paul wanted all his contemporaries to do: recognize every seeming folly, apparent contradiction, and real stumbling block as "the power of God and the wisdom of God." They will live by faith and never be surprised by Your often surprising ways. You will use them, as You use Your closest friends: in ways they never expected to be used; and they will rejoice in their hearts that they are not only being used by God but being of some use to God. When things are at their worst, humanly speaking, these people will be saying in their hearts what they said with their minds and lips in morning Mass: "mindful not only of the blessed Passion . . . but also of the Resurrection and Ascension." Then, like Christ, they will "endure the cross *because of the joy* set before them."

Dear God, do simplify life and living for them by allowing them to appreciate Mass. Let them see that the host used in today's Mass yielded its substance so that Your Son might be present among us in sacramental and sacrificial form. But that for tomorrow's Mass I will need another host. Then they will see that today's joys, sorrows, successes, and failures can serve as "wheat, water, and wine" for today's living of their Mass, but that for tomorrow's living of the same they will need different failures, successes, sorrows, and joys. Thus they will go along from day to day making Mass their life and their lives Mass; spiraling up ever closer and closer to You and Your Christ. The simplification will sublimate to this: for His Sacrifice Christ needed His own Flesh and Blood; for their "Sacrifice" they need nothing more. They need but hold themselves out to You and say: "This is Your Body. This, Your Blood." You will take them and "transubstantiate" them. Let them live that way, God, and their every heartbeat will go on saying the same thing over and over again without repeating itself once. It will be saying: "My God I love You. I am all Yours. Take me, and make me ever more like unto Yourself." It will never repeat itself, God, for each new heartbeat will be newer, greater, more generous love. That, dear God, is the message of Mass, as I hear it. That is what I would have become the song of their lives!

I told them in the beginning, God, that I was writing for the same reason St. John wrote: "that their joy might be full." Mass will do that; for in that "exchange" they will be made what they are: human sacredness; for their living will be naught but pulsating God-life. That sacredness will make their lives all love; for You are Love; and love brings JOY.

There it is, God: the answer. They should be getting more JOY in living "in Christ Jesus"; they should be knowing the bliss of touching Holiness and being transformed by that touch into "the holiness of God"; for Mass is not only holding God in our hands, but also placing ourselves into Your hands, and being carried by You into the Holy of Holies which we name the Sacred Heart of Jesus.

That is life, dear God. That is living. That is Mass. For that is LOVE.